GW01086798

THE NORMAN THOMPSON FILE

The History of the Norman Thompson Flight Company

and White & Thompson Ltd

Michael H. Goodall

An Air-Britain Publication

Published in Great Britain by

Air-Britain (Historians) Ltd
12 Lonsdale Gardens, Tunbridge Wells, Kent

Correspondence to:

J.J.Halley, 5 Walnut Tree Road,
Shepperton, Middlesex, TW17 ORW
and not to the Tonbridge address

ISBN 0 85130 233 5

Printed by Unwin Brothers Ltd
The Gresham Press
Old Woking
Surrey
GU22 9LH

Cover painting by Cliff Minney

CONTENTS

The original White & Thompson sheds at Middleton, Sussex

FOREWORD

When the author of this book sought me out in his researches for this account of my father's company's contribution to the development of practical flying craft, I knew he must inevitably find himself edging into records of a very offensive morass of double-dealing, selfishness and factitious obtuseness in various officials and private individuals. From that morass my father could only escape as an exile with loss of all prospect of continuing to work in his country's industry and of keeping the esteem of those of his family who could have afforded him help in re-establishing himself in professional engineering.

It would thus be all too possible for that morass, dominant as it was in the company's growth and decline, to have engulfed in this account of it any detail of its actual products and engineering achievement. But the author has sensed this risk and we are not bogged down in chicanery, legal or not, for more than a chapter or so; mostly this book reports, in commendable detailed recall, on the products and achievements for which the company should justly and always occupy a niche in the history of aviation and its pioneers like F.W.Lanchester and Norman Thompson. At last we have the Thompson flying-boats presented for themselves, the finest sea- and air-worthy craft of a line of development that culminated in the likes of Sunderland and Catalina before the era of the flying-boat faded in the face of the competition from jet-engined aeroplanes ranging far and fast enough across ocean or wilderness to do without waterborne landings.

In the heyday of production of the N.T.2B, a work's foreman made a 1/15th scale model of one in solid mahogany for my mother for Christmas 1918. Throughout the family's exile in France, "Daddy's aeroplane" hung in the hall of our home so that we children knew a flying-boat from a seaplane well before most of the grown-ups appearing in the Norman Thompson Flight Co. court cases. Throughout many removals and attic clearances this N.T.2B has survived, in more and more pieces as times passed. Latterly I have restored it to its original state and am surprised to find how pleasurable it instructs me as it polishes the memory of a pioneer aircraft designer too long remembered (if at all) for government victimisation rather than for any original technical prowess.

So too, I hope, will others, as I do, enjoy the revealing gleam of early aircraft history that Mike Goodall has so excellently brought out in this account of the contribution to that history of the White and Thompson/Norman Thompson Flight Company.

Oliver Norman Thompson

The Norman Thompson No.1 Biplane

INTRODUCTION

Following the publication in 1973 of my "Wight Aircraft" book and the very favourable comments by reviewers and the aviation world in general, I resolved to find an equally interesting company whose history had not previously been published in detail. After some searching I decided that White and Thompson might be a suitable subject and I commenced research in depth.

Initially all the usual sources were consulted and visits were made to the Middleton, Bognor and Littlehampton areas, but the trail was very cold and, not surprisingly, some sixty years after the closure of the Company, there were very few surviving local residents with first-hand knowledge of the site, the staff and the aircraft.

A visit to Somerset House to read Norman Thompson's will revealed the fact that he had had three children, one of whom, Oliver Norman, was described as an engineer. Contact with all the Engineering Institutes failed to trace him and I thought that I was out of luck. However, a sudden inspiration led me to look through all the United Kingdom telephone directories for an O. N. Thompson. Surprisingly, there was only one listed and a quick telephone call confirmed that I had struck gold. Mr.Thompson had many of his father's papers and photographs and was delighted to make them available to me. He had never expected that the sorry story of his father's shabby treatment would be retold but had always wished for better and lasting recognition of Norman Thompson's standing as a very sound development engineer worthy of his friendship and collaboration with such men as F.W.Lanchester and Henri Coanda in original applications of aero and fluid dynamics.

After studying the papers, it was very soon apparent that there was much more involved than just a straightforward aircraft company history. There was also a saga of commercial and government intrigue which led to the ruin of the company and a corruption case involving one of Britain's best-known and highly respected Naval airmen.

There is an old business adage that to be successful you must be lucky as well as clever. Unfortunately, luck always seems to have eluded Norman Thompson.

In an attempt to make the White and Thompson story interesting to the general reader I have avoided including a great deal of very technical data in the main body of the text. I would refer the more technically-minded reader to the various Appendices which appear at the end of the book.

Norman Thompson (on left) and Douglas White with the No.1 Biplane almost complete

CHAPTER 1

Norman Thompson, Douglas White and the founding of the firm.

Norman Arthur Thompson was born at Streatham on 28th March 1874, the son of Arthur Thompson, a well-to-do tea and rubber broker in the City of London. After preparatory school education, he was sent to Harrow in Summer 1888 and left in March 1891. In October 1891, he entered Trinity College, Cambridge, where he studied Mathematics and Science and Electrical Engineering for four years, eventually graduating as a B.A. in 1895. Two years' service with the General Electric Company in the United States was followed by employment with A.E.G. in Berlin and British Thompson-Houston in Rugby. During 1902/3, he was manager of the Clyde Valley Electrical Power Company until Westinghouse acquired financial control.

An academic interest in aerodynamics was crystallised by chance when, in 1907, his bookseller sent Thompson a copy of F.W.Lanchester's new book "Aerodynamics" which dealt with the fundamentals of flight, both as concerns lift and stability. A second volume, "Aerodonetics", followed in 1908. Lanchester's "tour-de-force" gave Thompson everything he needed of fundamental importance relating to the problems of mechanical

flight; it fired him with enthusiasm to become involved with the new science of aeronautics and to devote his life to aircraft design and manufacture. To this end, early in 1909, he decided to find a partner and therefore enlisted the aid of an old Trinity College friend, Doctor John White, ¶ with whom he approached Lanchester to discuss his plans. Lanchester's initial response was one of scepticism and he told them they would certainly lose their money. However, when Thompson explained how far Britain had lagged behind other countries in the development of the industry of the future - aviation - and that Doctor White was willing to finance an experimental machine, Lanchester realised that their motives were public-spirited and not just commercial. He therefore agreed to be their aeronautical consultant from 31st March 1909.

In August 1909, Lanchester and Thompson visited the great flying meeting at Reims and studied a variety of machines which were competing there. On their return, Lanchester commenced the design of a biplane, based largely on the ideas incorporated in his Patent 3608 of 1897, and work was put in hand with the Daimler Company of Coventry, for which he was engineering consultant.

At the same time, Thompson and Lanchester made many visits to the South Coast to view possible sites for a flying ground where experimental work could be carried out. Eventually what seemed to be a perfect location was found about midway between Littlehampton and Bognor at Middleton-on-Sea. Here the foreshore consisted of several miles of good firm sand, about three or four hundred yards wide at low tide and free from obstruction of any kind, not even seaweed. The sand had a very gradual slope, which drained well, and all-in-all it seemed an ideal site. Sheds and an office building were erected 20 or 30 yards above the high-water mark and a slipway was built leading out on to the sands. Thompson and Doctor White installed themselves at Middleton early in 1910 and recruited a small workforce; the firm of White and Thompson was now in being. Suitable machinery was installed and the fuselage of the first aeroplane was brought down from Daimlers for completion. By now the total staff numbered ten and new and larger offices and a bungalow for the watchman were built. The old office was turned into a storeroom and electric lighting was installed.

At this time, it was found that the ground was prone to flooding at high spring tides and, before the coastal defences were improved, the buildings were flooded on several occasions.

The first machine, the Thompson-Lanchester No.1, although in some ways many years in advance of its contemporaries, was dogged by that bad luck which was never far away from so many of Norman Thompson's aeronautical endeavours and was eventually so badly damaged by crashing on to rocks that it was scrapped. This must have been sometime in 1911 and, by now, Doctor White had reached the limit of the amount of money he was prepared to invest in work of an experimental nature. It was therefore decided to concentrate on more commercial activities which would, hopefully, bring in a return on the capital employed. As this was outside the terms on which he had joined the partnership, Lanchester resigned as aeronautical consultant in September 1913, although he continued to visit Middleton from time to time to watch progress. An additional reason for Lanchester leaving was that he had been appointed as a founder member of the Advisory Committee for Aeronautics in 1909 and felt that as a member of a Government body it was perhaps not proper for him to be associated with a firm actively engaged in the aeronautical industry.

White and Thompson was registered as a private limited company on 8th June 1912 "to take over as a going concern the business of aeroplane construction and aviation experts now carried on at Middleton, Bognor, under the style or firm of White and Thompson". The authorised capital was £20,000 in £1 shares and the Directors and initial subscribers were:

Douglas White	-	9,000 shares
Norman Thompson	-	2,000 shares
Arthur Thompson	-	500 shares
Charles Wolrycle Dixon	-	500 shares

The registered office was Aeronautic Works, Middleton.

Subsequently, Arthur Bonsor, a Littlehampton fishmonger, was made a director.

Norman Thompson

¶ John Douglas Campbell White was born in 1872 and after schooling at Charterhouse he went to Trinity College, Cambridge, in 1891, where he gained a First in the Classical Tripos and also in the Theological Tripos. He went on to qualify as a Doctor of Medicine and thereafter went into practice in Harrow and married in 1898. He retired from full-time practice in 1909 at the age of 37 on succeeding to the estates in Dunbartonshire of his uncle, Lord Overtoun. Thereafter, apart from a spell with the R.A.M.C. in World War One, he engaged in business and in various public and charitable works. He died in Harrow on 25th March 1940.

Frederick William Lanchester in 1894 with one of his first aeroplane models

CHAPTER 2

Lanchester and the "Grey Angel"

Frederick William Lanchester was born in Lewisham on October 28, 1868 and received his training in engineering at the Normal School of Science. By 1891 he was Works Manager of T.B.Barker's gas engine factory at Saltley and had started investigating the problems of flight. In 1892 he experimented with model gliders in the garden of his house at Olton, Birmingham and, in 1893, he built a large glider, six feet long, of white pine and pitch pine with lead ballast and weighing 1 lb 7 oz. This was followed by an elastic-powered version, seven foot long and weighing 2 ½lb with twin propellers. An elastic catapult was used to launch it at more than 40 m.p.h. In 1895, he spent many hours launching a variety of small gliders made of paper and mica from the upper windows of his house at Alvechurch. All these experiments were to observe various design features which induced automatic stability.

In 1893 he wrote a paper entitled "The Soaring of Birds and the Possibilities of Mechanical Flight" which outlined his theory of lift and drag and a review of available sources of power and in 1897 he submitted a further paper to the Physical Society for publication. Unfortunately it was rejected and, in an effort to publicise his theories of the flow round three-dimensional wings and the calculation of induced drag, he filed a patent specification (3608/1897). The patent drawing shows many of the features which, thirteen years later, were to find expression in the only full-size aeroplane designed by Lanchester, the Thompson-Lanchester No.1 Biplane, known to the workforce and local inhabitants as *The Grey Angel¶*. The patent confirms that Lanchester fully appreciated the need for streamlining "..I arrange a body of elongated and preferably streamline form of suitable dimensions to contain the propelling and other mechanisms and to provide sufficient accommodation for whatever purpose required". For high aspect ratio - "The

The Piggott No.1 Biplane of 1910 which incorporated many of Lanchester's ideas

form of wing employed to support the weight of the machine is preferably that of a soaring bird, that is to say of great lateral breadth and small fore and aft dimensions" - most desirably a ratio of from 10:1 to 13:1. For stability and control - "..the tailplane acting in conjunction with the supporting wings has for its principal functions the preservation of Longitudinal equilibrium and the regulation of speed, whilst the fins are concerned with the maintenance of transverse equilibrium and control of geographic direction; the inclination of the course of the horizontal is under the control of the propeller thrust" i.e. speed is controlled by use of the elevator and flight path angle by adjustment of thrust. "The lateral steering may be affected by means of a rudder or one of the fins may be used as a rudder, or an alteration in the angle of the two wings relatively to one another or parts of them will, by giving a list sideways to the machine, effect an alteration of its course" - a clear anticipation of the use of ailerons or wing warping.

In 1905, Lanchester was living in Hagley Road, Birmingham and resumed experiments with small gliders made of mica weighing between ½-gramme and 5 grammes to observe stability of flight. In 1905/7 he conducted experiments on skin friction and, in September 1908, he went to Göttingen, Berlin, Leipzig and Paris to increase his knowledge of aeronautics. Whilst in France he visited the Voisin factory and met Wilbur Wright at Le Mans. His two fundamental works on Aerodynamics and

Aerodonetics were published in 1907 and 1908.

After agreeing to help White and Thompson in their aeronautical venture, Lanchester drew up the specification for a single-seat high performance machine with a 50 h.p.Gnôme engine, to be capable of 90 m.p.h. The gross weight, including pilot and fuel, was to be about 800 lb. Lanchester had hoped that, with a single-seater machine which was inherently stable so that the pilot could use a gun or a camera and make visual observations, he would be able to keep the weight, power and cost to a minimum. However, before construction started, it was discovered that the War Office would only be interested in aeroplanes which could carry both pilot and observer. As at that time the Government appeared to be the main prospective buyer, it was decided that the design would have to be modified - the body was lengthened to accommodate a second seat behind the pilot. At that time there was no reliable engine of sufficient power to cope with the additional weight, so the design was altered to take two 50 h.p. Gnôme engines which were linked by a crossed belt running round flanged pulleys. The purpose of this was to equalise the propeller thrusts and to prevent drag and swing in the event of a complete failure of one engine. By now the design weight had risen to 1200/1300 lb. and the estimated maximum speed had dropped to 75 m.p.h.

The fuselage, built by Daimlers, followed conventional automobile constructional practice of those days - a framework of ash was covered with

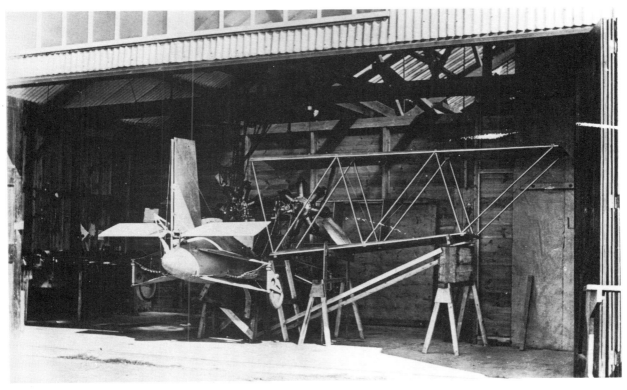

The Thompson-Lanchester No.1 Biplane being assembled at Middleton in 1910

mild steel plates, hand-beaten to shape.

The wings, made at Middleton, consisted of a main spar at about 40% of the chord from the leading edge and a second spar forming the leading edge, with main and secondary ribs which were sheathed above and below with 23 IWG high tension aluminium alloy sheet. The aluminium was riveted, following the practice of embossing the metal into counter-sink and the skin formed a perfect streamline section and a wing of considerable strength.

The box-kite type tailplane was a wooden framework covered in 26 gauge aluminium, pivoted at the rear of the fuselage and provided with a screw control whereby the incidence could be varied by the pilot. A small elevator was fitted in front for use in landing and taking off and for rapid manoeuvring in flight. The rudder was also mounted in the nose. Small ailerons were fitted to the outermost wing struts. The biplane structure was trussed by means of tubular steel struts in a W configuration.

The original landing mechanism was a hydraulically controlled pneumatic bolster invented by Lanchester (Patent 18384/1909) but this frequently became choked with sand and seaweed and was soon replaced by four wheels mounted on outriggers and restrained by springs which gave independent suspension. A claw-type drag brake was fitted under the rear of the body.

The original pusher propellers of 5 ft. 2 in. diameter were four-bladed, the sheet steel blades

being rivetted quite crudely to steel tube which was fitted into a cross-shaped central hub. It would seem that the pitch of the blades could be altered on the ground to vary the amount of thrust.

The Biplane was now complete but before it could leave its shed for trials, the firm was confronted with the first of the many setbacks which were to dog its progress. The beautiful expanse of firm sand was stripped away by a series of violent storms in which thousands of tons of sand disappeared, exposing stumps of the piling of old groynes and patches of chalk and rock. The levels of the beach were altered so that the receding sea left pools of water and mud and seaweed was everywhere. However, in spite of the unsuitable ground, the trials had to proceed and Norman Thompson, who seems to have had no previous flying experience, piloted the new machine himself. Initial taxying trials resulted in the undercarriage modifications mentioned above but unfortunately the outriggers were not strengthened and on the first attempt at a take-off on the very rough beach, the wheels on one side collapsed, the machine ground-looped and ended up on its back. Luckily Thompson was strapped into his seat with one of the White and Thompson patent safety-belts and escaped without injury. The strength of the structure was proved by the very small amount of damage sustained; apart from the twisted undercarriage there were just a few bent interplane struts and propeller blades.

The *Grey Angel* was taken back to its shed for

The No.1 Biplane complete outside its shed

repairs; the wing struts were straightened and the undercarriage was modified and strengthened. New three-bladed propellers were fitted. Further flights were attempted and various modifications were incorporated, including different wing bracing struts and a new type of three-bladed propeller.

During the flight trials, employees of the firm had to run along the shore chasing the machine and carrying planks to put under the wheels when it stopped to prevent it sinking into the soft sand. The unsuitable terrain and the high wing loading (12-12 ½lb/square foot) made the chance of a successful take-off fairly remote. At this time the test pilot was Captain Wilmot Nicholson R.N., the Captain Superintendent of Torpedo Boat Destroyers building by contract; based at the Admiralty, he travelled from London to Middleton to conduct the trials during 1911.

In spite of various further modifications and repairs, Nicholson was unable to persuade the "Grey Angel" to fly and it was eventually scrapped. The remains are said to have been dumped into a local duck pond, the present location of which is unknown.

Lanchester always felt that if the original design, with its lighter weight, had been adhered to, the chances of success would have been greater and the machine might have flown before half of Doctor White's money had been used up. He held the opinion that experimental work should be carried out without too much concern for its final commercial application and that the customer should not have too much opportunity to force the incorporation of a variety of modification to the original design - a problem which has bedevilled the British aircraft industry ever since!

SPECIFICATION

Engines: Two 50 h.p. Gnôme - built by Seguin of Paris. (One of these was No.11.)

Span Top:	25 ft.0 in.;
Bottom:	c 20 ft.0 in.
Chord, Top:	2 ft.6 in.;
Bottom:	2 ft.6 in.
Wing Area:	c 105 square feet
Aspect ratio:	Top: 10:1 Bottom: 8:1
Length:	c 14 feet
Cruising speed:	75 m.p.h.
Gross weight:	c 1,200 lb.

¶ The large biplane designed by S.C.Parr and built by Piggott Brothers and Company in 1910 incorporated a number of Lanchester's ideas.

The No.1 Biplane with modified interplane struts tethered for thrust measurement

The No.1 Biplane after its final crash. Note the wingtip ailerons and the rake-type brake under the fuselage. The wheel fairings have been removed

13

These photographs show clearly the four-bladed propellers fitted at the time of the crash

The Norman Thompson No.1 Biplane on 9th January 1913

CHAPTER 3

The Norman Thompson No.1 Biplane

After the departure of Lanchester and the disappointing trials of the Thompson-Lanchester No.1 Biplane, Norman Thompson set out to design a two-seater biplane which would have both military and civilian potential and which would incorporate several new constructional methods, in particular the patented metal wing designs outlined in full in Appendix IV. Briefly, these consisted of wings with metal ribs and spars and steel wires stretched spanwise between wing-root and wing-tip. The fabric covering was threaded in and out between the wires; thin aluminium sheet could also be used.

The Norman Thompson No.1 emerged at the beginning of January 1913 as a pusher biplane with sheet steel-covered body, fabric-covered wings, tubular steel tail-booms and struts and fabric-covered tailplane and rudder.

The two-seater cockpit was at the extreme rear of the short fuselage just in front of the three-bladed all-steel propeller.

The undercarriage incorporated an improved arrangement of elastic suspension and method of attachment to the body of the machine so as to diminish shocks and stresses in different directions and to prevent a breakage of the undercarriage from extending to the body structure. The arrangements were covered by Patent No.23744 of 1912.

The 100 h.p. water-cooled A.B.C. engine was mounted well forward and low down on the fuselage and was linked to the propeller by a long drive-shaft which passed between the two-man crew. The drive arrangement was covered by Patent No.12655 of 1912. A large radiator was mounted in the extreme nose and the fuel tank was positioned between the engine and the cockpit. The high-mounted position of the fuel tank gave an adequate flow of fuel to the engine without the necessity of a fuel-pump.

Small wheels, with unusually large (for that

The Norman Thompson No.1 Biplane

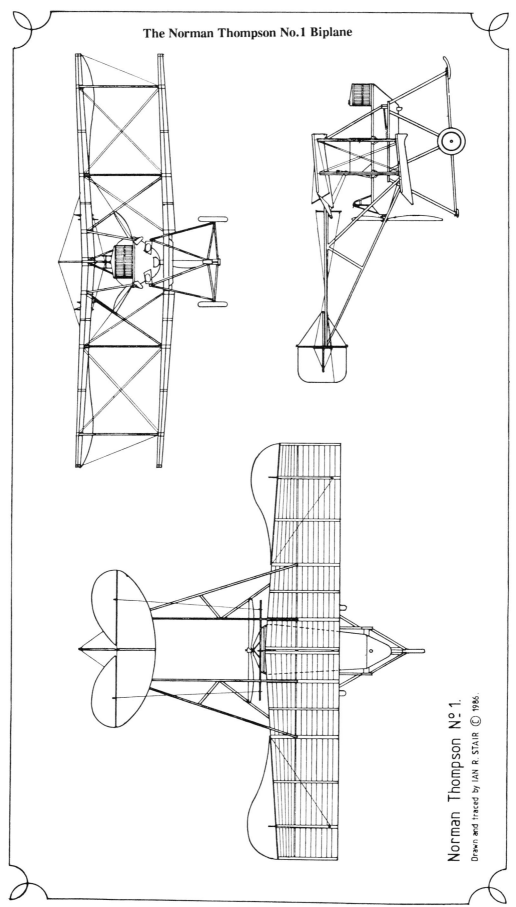

Norman Thompson Nº 1.

Drawn and traced by IAN R. STAIR © 1986.

The Norman Thompson No.1 Biplane. Note wing construction and three-bladed propeller

period) low-pressure tyres, were fitted to the tubular steel undercarriage in conjunction with a central single skid.

Ailerons of sheet fibre were initially fitted to the top wings only, but were subsequently added to the lower wings as well.

Test flying was carried out from Middleton sands by E.R.Whitehouse, R.L.Charteris and John Porte and proved to be quite successful with a short take-off and fairly high top speed. Norman Thompson also flew the little biplane during the Summer of 1913. It was finally badly damaged by Porte when he collided with a pile of rocks early in 1914. By then, White and Thompson were preoccupied with Curtiss flying boats and the Biplane was not repaired.

SPECIFICATION

Type:	Norman Thompson No.1 Biplane
Date:	1913-1914
Seats:	Two
Power:	100 h.p.A.B.C. 4-cylinder water-cooled
Span:	About 30 ft
Root chord:	About 4 ft.5 in.
Gap:	About 5 ft.5 in.
Fuselage length:	About 9 ft.
Propeller:	About 8 ft.9 in. diameter
Wheels:	About 1 ft.7 in. diameter

ABC engine fitted and ailerons on lower wing

Side view of No.1 Biplane

The Bass-Curtiss Airboat

CHAPTER 4

The Curtiss Flying Boats

Glenn Hammond Curtiss set up business at Hammondsport, New York, towards the end of the 19th Century as a builder of bicycles. Within a year or two he was fitting small engines to the machines and before long he was building engines to his own design. His motorcycles were very successful and his racing prowess spread far beyond the borders of New York State. Eventually, in 1904, he was asked to build a special engine for Thomas Baldwin's airship. This early involvement with aviation led in 1907 to his being invited to join the Aerial Experiment Association as director of experiments and the various machines designed by the Association were built at the Curtiss works at Hammondsport.

After the winding up of the A.E.A. in 1909, Curtiss continued to build aircraft to his own design and, in spite of a running fight with the Wright Brothers over the alleged infringement of their patents, the firm prospered and, by 1913, it was the largest manufacturer of aircraft in the United States.

Curtiss's first experience with waterborne aircraft was the twin-float *Loon* designed by the A.E.A. and built in 1908. Although unsuccessful, it led directly to the Canoe machine of 1910 and a whole series of generally successful seaplanes and

flying boats. By 1913, a range of Model E and Model F Flying Boats was in service with the U.S. Army and Navy and various private owners.

During 1911 Curtiss had opened a flying school for hydro-aeroplanes at North Island, San Diego, California and the virtually-guaranteed good weather attracted pupils from as far afield as Europe. Ernest C. Bass was a wealthy young man who was related to the Bass brewing family and to Waterlows the printers. Round about the turn of the century, he went to America to find adventure; a spell as an amateur bullfighter in Mexico was followed by service with the Texas Rangers, in which he rose to the rank of Captain, a title he used for the rest of his life. The advent of flying in the United States soon attracted him and he made the acquaintance of several of the pioneer flyers, including Glenn Curtiss, with whom he became very friendly. Bass eventually learned to fly in America, very possibly at the Curtiss School.

The expansion of flying activity in England had mainly taken place on land; the limited amount of flying from water had been with float seaplanes, flying boats being almost unknown. Bass, having learned of the success of the Curtiss Model E and F flying boats in America, contacted Curtiss in the

Glenn Curtiss (on left), John Porte (centre) and Loftus Bryan (on right) with the Curtiss Model F at Volk's Seaplane Station at Brighton

Summer of 1913 and persuaded him to bring some of his latest boats to England for a demonstration and sales tour.

As related more fully in Chapter 13, Lieutenant John C.Porte had learnt to fly at Reims and gained his French Aero Club certificate on 28 July 1911. By this time he had been invalided out of the Royal Navy with tuberculosis. Following a successful season as a racing pilot, Porte teamed up with Lawrence Santoni to form the British Deperdussin Company to build Deperdussin aeroplanes for the British market. Their production included a seaplane

the *Seagull*. The Company went into liquidation in August 1913 and Porte was invited by Bass to join the syndicate which had been formed to bring the Curtiss boats to England. Magnus and Hermann Volk, prolific inventors and owners of the electric railway along the seashore at Brighton, had set up a seaplane station on the beach near Paston Place the previous Summer. They agreed to its use by the syndicate to demonstrate Curtiss flying boats and a large marquee tent was erected on the shingle to provide protection for the aircraft using this primitive seaplane station. Curtiss and his Model F

The Curtiss Triad off Bognor

Volk's Seaplane Station on the beach at Brighton

19

Curtiss "English" Model F. Note aileron mounted on top wing

boat arrived at Brighton in the middle of October 1913 and two pilots, Lieutenant Loftus Bryan and Eric Gordon-England, assisted in the erection of the Model F. White and Thompson were appointed as repairers for the syndicate and it appears possible that Curtiss brought over a *Triad* seaplane as one was photographed off Bognor at about this time.

The Model F was fitted with a 100 h.p.Curtiss OX5 engine driving a two-bladed pusher propeller. As with the majority of Curtiss aircraft at that time, the Model F was fitted with mid-gap ailerons. The control system was unusual. The left-hand seat had the usual type of Curtiss control with an armchair, the upper part of which moved from side to side as the pilot moved his body and thus operated the ailerons; the rudder was controlled by a wheel and the elevators by a fore and aft movement of the control column. The right-hand seat was equipped with a control column and wheel which operated the ailerons and elevators and a foot-bar connected to the rudder. The machine could therefore be flown by pilots who were used to either type of control. The fore-part of the hull in front of the cockpit was hinged to fold forward to allow easy access to the seats and the inside of the hinged portion was lined with rubber matting which made a non-slip walkway along the nose of the boat.

Observers from the aeronautical press commented on the excellent workmanship of the Model F, but this opinion was not shared by Norman Thompson, who some years later wrote:

"By way of illustrating more clearly the state of flying boat construction before the design of the

Porte and Curtiss

Side view of the Curtiss "English" Model F

"N.T.2", the difficulties to be encountered and the defects to be avoided, a summary is given below of the leading defects disclosed to Mr. Norman Thompson and two pilots acting for his firm, the late Commander J.C. Porte R.N., C.M.G. and Flight Lieutenant E.R. Whitehouse, when testing the 90 h.p. Curtiss model during the winter of 1913-14 at the works of Messrs. White & Thompson Ltd near Bognor.

It should be explained that Mr. Thompson had acquired for his firm, then known as White & Thompson Ltd., the exclusive agency rights for Great Britain for the flying boats, aeroplanes and engines of the Curtiss Aeroplane Co. of New York. A thorough examination and testing of the latest model of "Curtiss" flying boat at that date was therefore of particular interest to his firm.

(1) The hull constantly leaked, was too weak to stand even moderate landing shock on the water without some of the timbers cracking and showed no sign of being built by anyone with a knowledge of boat construction.

(2) The wings contained no internal bracing to take the head resistance of "drift" stresses. Reliance was placed exclusively on external wires of doubtful strength from the prow of the boat to points on the front of the planes to prevent the wings folding backwards under the wind pressure, for instance in a nose dive. The whole wing construction was weak, as was evidenced in a 90 h.p. Curtiss Flying-boat which had a bad accident at Antibes in the spring of 1914 and was sent to the writer's works for repair and new wings.

(3) The tail structure contained no element to take the torsional or side stresses, which tend to twist the tail structure round the stern of the hull and wrench it's (sic) fixings.

(4) The bracing and control wires of the machine were found to be so inadequate due to size, materials and methods of connection, that both the writer and the late Commander Porte condemned the machine as unfit for further flying until re-wired in a secure and safe manner.

(5) The vertical post supporting the rudder-bar carried away with Lieutenant Whitehouse - fortunately when he had only just left the water a few feet. It appeared that the points of the 3 wood screws supposed to secure the foot of the post to the floor only penetrated about one eighth of an inch into the wood floor and the latter was constantly sodden with water.

(6) The robust looking strut sloping backwards from a point on the keel in the cockpit up to the front of the engines, intended to keep the latter from coming forward on to the pilot in a smash, was so weakly fixed that it's lower end invariably slid along the keel from the ordinary shocks due to planing on the water, while it's upper attachment showed an equal lack of mechanical conception. This strut was referred to in the Royal Naval Air Service as "the strut which went from nowhere to nowhere"."

This strut, always known as the "Goodier strut"

Curtiss Model F being beached at Brighton

or "bow strut", was fitted to all Model F and subsequent Curtiss boats following a crash landing on 18 February 1913 in which Lieutenant Lewis Goodier Jr. was seriously injured. The engine, lacking any fore and aft bracing, had torn loose from its bearers and had crushed Lieutenant Goodier against the control column and dashboard.

Gordon-England was equally unimpressed when taken for a flight by the American pilot Earl Cooper in October or November 1913. He commented: "it was absolutely unstable in every direction and badly put together - it frightened me stiff".

It was the realisation of the defects of the Curtiss flying boat enumerated above which first led Norman Thompson to design and produce the White and Thompson No.2 Flying Boat.

The demonstrations at Brighton attracted great interest and numbers of well-known people in the aviation world attended the Volk's site to watch the flying and to examine the Curtiss. These included Harold Perrin, Secretary of the Royal Aero Club, Gordon Bell, Moorhouse, Morison, Porte, Delacombe and Marechal. The German Navy was represented by Captain von Pustau and another officer.

Glenn Curtiss returned to America at the end of October 1913, having given the sole agency for the sale in Europe of his flying boats and engines to Ernest Bass, assisted by John Porte. White and

Thompson were confirmed as official repairers. The headquarters of the agency was initially at the Royal Albion Hotel at Brighton. Flights were carried out all along the South Coast to demonstrate the boat and the reliability of its engine. In November 1913, it was flown by Porte and Cooper to Middleton where its control system was changed totally from the Curtiss yoke to the Deperdussin type and for the installation of navigation instruments. Later that month and in early December, the demonstration flights and trials continued and during one of them it seems that damage occurred, as the boat went into the works of Hamble River, Luke and Company at Hamble for repair. At the same time the hull was varnished inside and out, which surprisingly had not been done in America. It is not known why this firm was used rather than White and Thompson but it is possible that the damage was too severe for the boat to be flown to Middleton. Another possibility is that the shed at Middleton was occupied by the Vickers E.F.B.2, which was carrying out flight trials from the beach there at the hands of Harold Barnwell, who flew down there in a Vickers Monoplane.

A second Curtiss Model F was imported in December 1913.

On 1 February 1914, Bass's sole agency for Curtiss flying boats and engines was transferred to White and Thompson, who were thereby to act as exclusive agents for the Curtiss Company in Great

The Bass-Curtiss Airboat

Britain and its Dominions for a period of twelve years. The Middleton works were thereafter increased in size and a flying boat training school was set up with John Porte as the instructor. Although Norman Thompson was not impressed by the workmanship or flying qualities of the Curtiss, he saw the agency as part of a policy of development for his company as designers and constructors of flying boats in this country.

After its repair, the Curtiss demonstration machine was flown from Hamble to Brighton and then back to Middleton. It was then sold to Captain Bass and packed up for transport to the French Riviera, where he proposed to spend several months and use the machine for sporting flying. Two additional boats were ordered from Curtiss, presumably for use at the White & Thompson flying school.

The first pupil of the school was Gerard Hudson who ultimately ordered two Curtiss flying boats from White and Thompson for delivery to South Africa, where he was to represent Curtiss's interests. However, Norman Thompson refused to complete the sale following poor reports by Whitehouse and Porte regarding the handling qualities and construction of the Curtiss-built machines.

Following this, it would seem that the Middleton team set to and designed and built an English version of the Model F which incorporated new wings with conventional ailerons on the top wing, stronger bracing and a strengthened hull. The hull was built up on ash frames set at 3 inch

intervals, to which were attached 1 inch ash longerons running the length of the hull. The sides of the hull were planked with two layers of mahogany with an interleaving layer of strong canvas set in marine glue. The hull was divided into eight watertight compartments. The new machine was completed by 27 March 1914 and was tested by John Porte who found that it would take off well from a choppy sea with a passenger.

Porte left White and Thompson in April and went to America to join Curtiss as potential pilot of a large flying boat being built for John Wanamaker for an attempt on the first crossing of the Atlantic by air.

Meanwhile Bass's Curtiss had crashed at Antibes and had been brought back to Middleton for repair. It emerged at the beginning of June with new wings of RAF6 section and fitted with a 100 h.p. Anzani radial engine. On trials with Whitehouse and Loftus Bryan in the middle of June, it showed a marked increase in speed as compared with when the original Curtiss wings were fitted. It was known as the "Bass-Curtiss Airboat".

Summer 1914 saw White and Thompson fully involved in preparing their two entries for the *Daily Mail* "Circuit of Britain" Race. In the event this was cancelled following the outbreak of war on 4 August. Within a day or two thereafter, officials from the Admiralty visited Middleton and impressed the two "Circuit of Britain" flying boats; a third machine, probably one of the original Curtiss boats, was ordered to be destroyed. It was stripped of its engine and fittings and then burned on the beach.

The Curtiss OX-5 engine in the Curtiss Model F

Meanwhile, at Hammondsport, John Porte had been extensively involved in not only the piloting of the large *America* flying boat but also giving considerable advice to Curtiss on the design of the hull and its construction. After the outbreak of the Great War necessitated the cancellation of the attempt on the Atlantic crossing, Porte returned to Britain at the beginning of August and, in spite of his long-standing illness, rejoined the Royal Naval Air Service. The *America* and a sister machine which had also been built were offered, at the instigation of Porte, to the British Admiralty as the Curtiss H.1. Porte's enthusiasm fort the large "America" flying boats led the Admiralty into direct negotiations with the Curtiss Company for the supply of improved versions, the H.2 and H.4, and very soon Curtiss became one of the principal manufacturers of British naval aircraft. Curtiss totally ignored their agreement with White and Thompson and, because of wartime secrecy, it was some time before the British company found out what was happening. Curtiss's attitude towards White and Thompson seems to have been similar to that of King George V's famous reply when asked if he would like to go to Bognor to recuperate following a serious illness. It was not until 3 February 1915 that Curtiss wrote attempting a one-sided termination of their agreement with White and Thompson. This underhanded action led directly to the Porte/Casson/Seeley corruption case of 1917 and to the destruction of the Norman Thompson Company, the story of which is told in Chapter 13.

Specification

Type:	Curtiss "F" Boat
Date:	1913/1914
Seats:	Two
Power:	100 h.p. Curtiss OX (Type "F")
	100 h.p. Anzani (Bass-Curtiss Airboat)
Span:	38 ft.4 in. (41 ft.8 in. with ailerons)
Length:	26 ft.0 in.
Chord:	5 ft.6 in.
Gap:	5 ft.6 in.

Type:	"English" Curtiss
Date:	1914
Seats:	Two
Power:	100 h.p. Curtiss OX
Span:	41 ft.0 in.
Length:	27 ft.4 in.
Chord:	5 ft.3 in.
Gap:	5 ft.6 in.
Wing area:	378 square feet

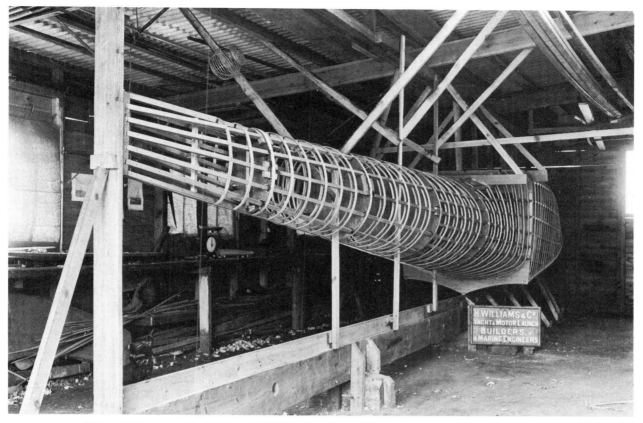

White & Thompson No. 1 Flying Boat under construction at H Williams & Co., Littlehampton

CHAPTER 5

The "Circuit of Britain" Flying Boats

Norman Thompson's ambition to produce a really successful flying boat, and an advance on the Curtiss machine, was given a fillip by the announcement by the *Daily Mail* of a 1914 "Circuit of Britain" Race for flying boats to be held in August. A twin-engined machine had already been laid down in March 1914 and it was decided that this would be one of the entries for the Race. A second entry was also designed; this was a single-seat two-seater, based on the "English" Curtiss.

The twin-engined machine, the White & Thompson No.1 Flying Boat, was effectively an enlarged version of the "English" Curtiss, fitted with two 90 h.p. Curtiss OX engines which were built by the Austin Motor Company under licence and driving three-bladed pusher propellers with adjustable pitch. The hull, boat-built of elm and spruce and planked with mahogany, was made at the Britannia Works of H.Williams & Company of Littlehampton. Williams were an old-established firm of yacht and motor-launch builders and marine engineers, who had their yard on the East bank of the River Arun. Williams eventually became a subsidiary of White & Thompson and built many of their flying-boat hulls.

The fore-part of the hull was of roughly rectangular section merging into a circular section aft of the single step. The spars of the lower wing passed through the top of the hull and were further braced by four steel tubes running from the base of the interplane struts to the lower sides of the hull. Large floats with springboard protectors were fitted at the wing-tips.

The engines were mounted on stout ash bearers supported on a triangulated structure of steel tubes which rested on the lower-wing main spars. Two additional struts ran forward from the engine mounting to the keel. Radiators for each engine were mounted on the front of the engine bearers.

Double-acting ailerons were hinged to the outer half of the upper-wing rear spar. The tail assembly was typically Curtiss in appearance, with a long fin running almost the whole length of the hull aft of the wings, with the tailplane mounted on top of the fin and braced to the hull. Additional fin area was provided by two large vertical surfaces fitted to the top wing just outboard of the engines.

The White & Thompson No.1 was to have been

The White and Thompson No.1

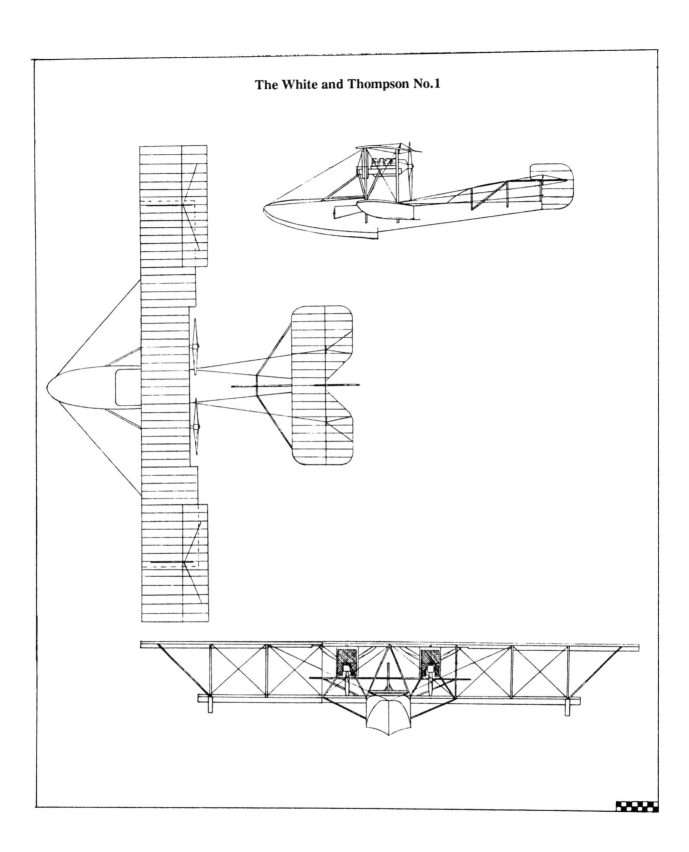

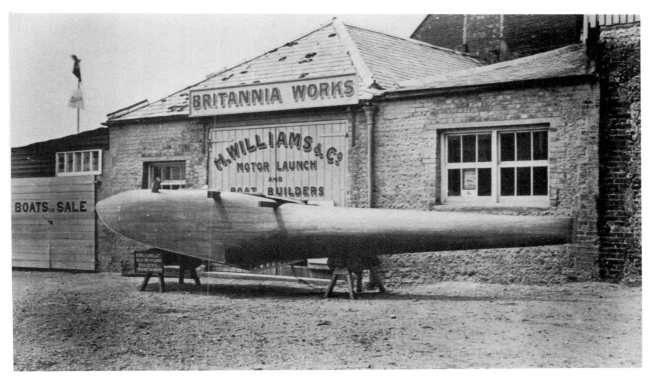

The completed hull of White & Thompson No.1 Flying Boat outside the Britannia Works

entry No.9 for the "Circuit of Britain" Race and its pilot would have been A.Loftus Bryan.

The Race was cancelled due to the outbreak of war on 4 August 1914 but it is very doubtful if the No.1 would have been able to compete as it had not flown by that time. It would seem that the Curtiss hull design was unsuitable for a machine of heavier weight and probable difference in centre of balance as compared with the smaller Curtiss flying boats.

Percy Hyde Beadle joined White & Thompson as chief designer on 10 August 1914 and in a letter to *"Flight"* in May 1918 he wrote:

With reference to the Letters Patent No.1256878 granted to Mr.Glenn H.Curtiss by the United States Patent Office recently published, it may interest your readers to be acquainted with the fact that a hull so constituted was built and tested by way of an experiment on the twin-engined White & Thompson Flying Boat which was destined for the Circuit of Britain Race to be held at the end of 1914, but postponed by the outbreak of war.

This machine was designed before I joined the above firm as chief designer, and on trial she refused to attain sufficient speed on the water to lift or even plane, and although I tried various means of curing the trouble, it was not until planing extensions or fins were built into the hull that this was effectively done.

The above experiments were carried out in September and the beginning of October 1914, and as witness thereto I can do no better than state that

Mr.E.C.Gordon England, now General Manager to Messrs.Sage Ltd, Peterborough, was pilot during all the above trials, and was accompanied by me, besides various members of Messrs. White & Thompson Ltd.

I therefore assume that all designers of flying-boats in this country who desire to use lateral planing fins on their hulls are quite at liberty to do so, as it was not until December 11th 1914, that Mr.Curtiss applied for his patent

Shortly after the outbreak of war, No.1 was impressed by the Admiralty and allocated serial number 883. It is possible that in Naval service it would have been fitted with two 100 h.p. Anzani engines (as were the Curtiss *America* boats) but no record has been found to indicate that it was actually ever delivered to the R.N.A.S.

Although unsuccessful and "forgotten" by Norman Thompson when he came to allocate N.T. numbers to all his designs, it paved the way for the later, reasonably successful, N.T.4, N.T.4a and N2c twin-engined flying boats built by the company. The single-engined machine, entry No.6 for the "Circuit of Britain", was a straight-forward improved version of the "English" Curtiss and was known as the White & Thompson No.2 Flying Boat. Presumably because Williams were fully occupied with the building of the hull of the No.1 Flying Boat, S.E.Saunders of Cowes were given a contract to build the hull of the No.2 and this appears to have been the start of a long association

No.1 Flying Boat at Middleton with Circuit of Britain Race No.9 on rudder

between the two firms.

The pilot for the race would have been Captain E.C.Bass.

The 24-foot hull was built up of two skins of copper-sewn mahogany "Consuta" plywood over a framework of ash and spruce and incorporated a single step just aft of the leading edge of the wing. A roomy cockpit forward of the wings accommodated pilot and passenger side-by-side and in front of them a decking curved upwards to form a wind-screen. Dual control was fitted and consisted of rotatable hand-wheels operating the elevators and ailerons and foot-bars for the rudders.

The rectangular wings were removed bodily from the Bass-Curtiss Airboat and had square-cut tips with considerable overhang on the top plane, which was braced by diagonal steel struts. Ailerons were fitted to the top wings only. A modified RAF6 wing section was used.

It was originally intended that the No.2 Flying Boat would be fitted with the 125 h.p. British Anzani engine, built by Coventry Ordnance Works, but when needed it was at Farnborough as an entry for the Government Engine Competition and was thus not available. A 120 h.p. Beardmore Austro-Daimler No.119 was therefore obtained on loan and was mounted on ash bearers which rested on a structure of steel tubes bolted to the lower-wing main spars. It drove a four-bladed pusher propeller. The trailing-edge of the upper-wing centre section was cut away to allow for clearance for the propeller. The radiator was mounted in front of the

engine, as was a small fuel tank to which petrol was pumped from the main tank which rested on the bottom of the hull.

A vertical fin was fixed above the top-wing centre section, wire-braced to the main spars, no doubt to counteract the large side area of the hull. In addition, a large fin extended forward from the rudder almost to the trailing-edge of the lower-wing. The lower portion of the rudder was metal covered and served as a water rudder when taxying. The tailplane was a simple rectangle with a cut-out for the rudder and was set at a negative angle of incidence. Two metal floats, of rectangular section, were attached under the lower-wing tips and were protected by sprung wooden boards.

The hull arrived from Saunders during the first week of July 1914 and was soon mated with the flight organs and engine. After completion, the White & Thompson No.2 was launched and made its first test flight on Friday 1st August with E.R.Whitehouse at the controls and a Mr.Dodds (Office Manager) as passenger. It left the water in 40 yards and performed very well. Further test flights were made but by now the gathering war clouds had forced the cancellation of the "Circuit of Britain". Captain Bass had offered his services to the Army and, shortly after the outbreak of war, Admiralty officials visited Middleton and commandeered the No.2 Flying Boat which, as No.882, went to Calshot on 7 August. Subsequently it went to the Isle of Grain Air Station for training and patrol duties and there became known as the

No.1 Flying boat under construction

Almost complete at Middleton

only seaplane which could be trusted to fly when wanted. From Grain it went to Felixstowe, where it gained the same good reputation. It was eventually wrecked there on 8 June 1915.

In his submission to the Commission on Awards to Inventors, Norman Thompson wrote the following description of the White & Thompson No.2, which, after the name of the company was changed on 21 September 1915 to The Norman Thompson Flight Company, was always known as the N.T.2:

"The first flying boat designed by Mr.Norman Thompson, tested 5 days before the war, and which had been intended to compete in the *Daily Mail* seaplane race round Britain, consisted, as regards general features, of a boat with a cockpit in front for the pilot and passenger, a pair of biplane wings, with a small stabilising float under each lower wing tip, mounted immediately behind, and a tail plane with elevators and rudder carried off the stern. The engine, an 120 h.p. Austro-Daimler, supplied by Messrs.Beardmore was mounted with its propeller between the upper and lower planes and supported from the boat.

So far the "N.T.2" resembles previous types of flying boats such as the "Curtiss" or "Donnet-Levêque", but the resemblance is entirely superficial. It is in the design and construction of the various essential parts and organs, as set out in detail below, that the "N.T.2" differed very sensibly from, and consequently proved a notable advance on, all previous flying boats.

Reference to the photographs and drawings will assist in appreciating the points in question.

A (as to performance)
(1)   As distinct from previous types, both lateral and fore and aft stability were so far automatic that the machine could be flown largely with hands off the controls.

(2)   When the engine was cut off during flight, the tail of the machine rose automatically putting the machine into the natural gliding position; whereas in the "Curtiss", for instance, and other previous types, unless the pilot at once used the elevator to force the machine's nose down, the machine would rear up and so lose sufficient speed to remain supported steadily in the air, and bring about considerable risk of a serious accident.

(3)   The machine banked at steep angles without side slip.

(4)   The speed attained was 85 m.p.h. - considerably in excess of previous types

B (as to construction)
(5)   The use of a wing whose profile, or section, when cut by a vertical fore and aft plane, was known as "R.A.F.6". This section was the result of experiments at the Royal Aircraft Factory, and was just available for use in 1914 when Mr.Thompson began designing the "N.T.2". It was the best known and contributed to the efficiency of "N.T.2"'s performance.

(6)   The tail plane was substantially a parallelogram in form and of "high aspect ratio", that is to say, with a span meeting the wind at least several times the fore and aft breadth. It was also mounted so as to be non-lifting, but to take a slightly negative load, the trailing edge of the tail plane during flight being normally a little above the level of the leading edge, the plane thus receiving top wind producing a downward pressure thereon. Mr.Thompson had personally always adopted the practice of a high aspect ratio non-lifting tail since seeing it's advantages set forth when reading Mr.F.W.Lanchester's work on "Aerial Flight" when it came out in 1908.

Norman Thompson with the No. 2 Flying Boat. Note the Circuit of Britain Race number 6 on rudder

The construction and setting of tail enabled the N.T.2 machine to take up her gliding position automatically when the engine was cut off, as alluded to above. It had not however been adopted in any previous flying boat, and in comparatively few flying machines of any kind at the date in question. The "Curtiss" tail plane was triangular in form with the apex leading to the wind and was consequently ineffective in giving fore and aft stability to the machine. The "Donnet-Levêque" was semi-elliptical with the semi major axis placed fore and aft and the curved edge leading to the wind; hence also inefficient for its purpose.

(7) Difficulty seems to have been experienced in previous types of flying boat in attaching the tail structure securely and firmly to the stern of the hull, particularly in regard to meeting the side stresses tending to twist the tail structure round the stern of the hull. In the "N.T.2" a suitable mechanical construction was devised to meet these requirements, whilst in the "Curtiss" the primary feature demanded by mechanics, viz. triangulation, to provide torsional stiffness of the tail structure round the hull, was absent.

(8) A vertical fin set centrally fore and aft above the top plane suitably formed and disposed in relation to the other surfaces and parts of the machine so as to give lateral stability, and permit steep banking without side slip, as referred to above.

(9) A boat of suitable lines and form to meet the required conditions built by Messrs. Saunders of Cowes of cedar sewn with copper wire on their well-known system which was strong enough to stand considerable pounding when planing at speed on the water without leaking.

(10) An engine mounting of streamline steel tubular framework so triangulated and constructed to carry the engine securely and rigidly on it's position between the upper and lower planes, and to obviate the strut of the "Curtiss" type from the front of the engine mounting down forwards to the keel of the hull in the pilot's cockpit, which was intended to keep the engine from coming forward on to the pilot in an accident of bad alighting.

(11) Complete elimination of well known defects in detail mechanical design, such as the method of attaching the end of a steel tube, which is liable to compressive stresses, to another structural element which it meets at an inclined angle by flattening the end of the tube, bonding this to lie flat against the element to which it is to be attached, boring a hole through it, and bolting it to the other structural member. This practice gives a weak though

The White and Thompson No.2

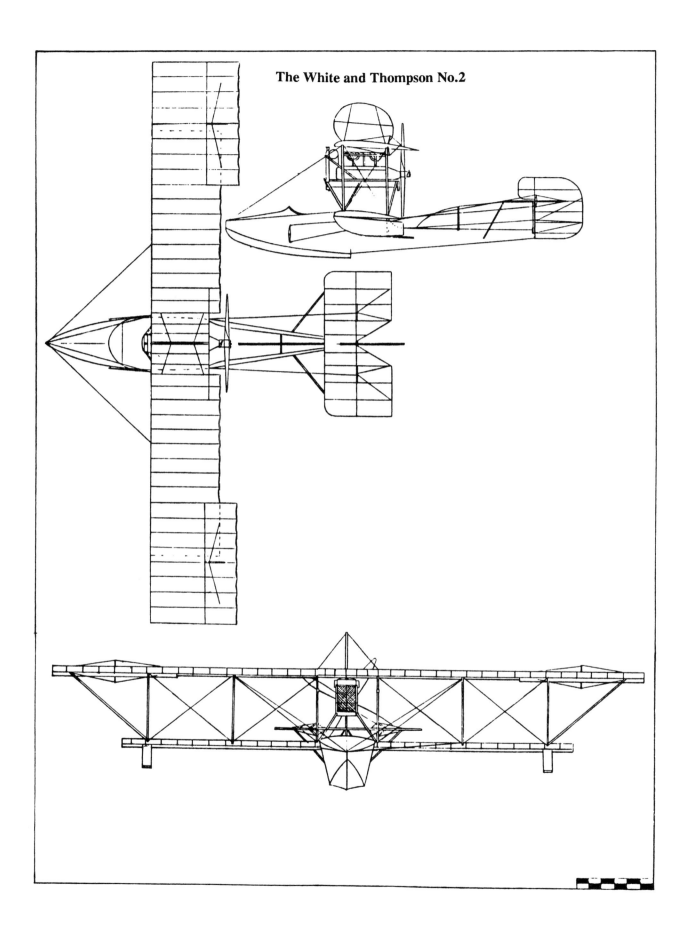

The White & Thompson No.2 Flying Boat completed at Middleton-on-Sea

cheap joint and asks for trouble, but was observable both in the "Sopwith" Bat Boat, a flying boat without a stern with the tail carried on spars from the main structure, built in 1913, and in the "Curtiss" flying boat of 1914.

It will be seen that the success of the "N.T.2" flying boat was due to a novel and effective combination of known features well designed and carried out.

Service History
No.882: Completed July 1914; first flight 1.8.14; Calshot 10.8.14; Grain 27.8.14; Felixstowe 10.11.14; wrecked Felixstowe 8.1.15; rebuilt Felixstowe 15.1.15; Felixstowe 12.3.15; side-slipped on landing and written off at Felixstowe 8.6.15

No.883 Not delivered by 31 August 1915

The Curtiss OX-5 engine

Specifications

Type:	W&T No.1	W&T No.2
Date:	1914-1915	1914-1915
Seats:	Two	Two
Power:	Two 100 h.p. Curtiss OX Two 100 h.p. Anzani ?	One 120 h.p. Beardmore Austro-Daimler No.119
Length:	32 ft.3 in.	27 ft.6 in.
Height:	c10 ft.6 in.	c11 ft.6 in.
Span: upper:	52 ft. 0 in.	45 ft. 0 in.
lower:	40 ft. 0 in.	34 ft. 0 in.
Chord:	5 ft.6 in.	5 ft. 6 in.
Gap:	c 5 ft.6 in.	5 ft. 9 in.
Stagger:	Nil	Nil
Tailplane span:	17 ft. 0 in.	12 ft. 0 in.
Tailplane chord:	6 ft. 3 in.	5 ft. 2 in.
Wing area:	500 sq feet	400 sq feet
Tailplane area:	97 sq feet	57 sq feet
Fin and rudder area:	30 sq feet	16 sq feet
Empty weight:	2,000 lbs	1,600 lbs
Loaded weight:	3,000 lbs	2,400 lbs
Max speed:	N/A	70 m.p.h.
Endurance	N/A	6 hours
Petrol capacity:	90 gallons	60 gallons
Production:	1 aircraft	1 aircraft
Serial No.	883	882
Contract:	CP53624/14	CP53624/14
Price:	N/A	£2,400

The White & Thompson No.3 in the harbour at Littlehampton

CHAPTER 6

The White & Thompson No.3, N.T.2 and N.T.2A Flying Boats

The success of the impressed No.2 Flying Boat soon led the Admiralty to place an order on 29 October 1914 for six examples of an improved version. Although this was the third W & T Flying Boat, it was later known to the Company as the N.T.2. The basic structure was virtually identical with that of the W & T No.2, but with minor alterations in detail design. The wing-tips were slightly rounded, the large fin fitted above the centre-section was replaced by two smaller fins above each pair of inboard interplane struts, the main fin area was slightly increased and an additional small fin was fitted above the tailplane. The upper-wing extensions were braced to "goal post" king posts. The engine was a 120 h.p. Beardmore Austro-Daimler with a car-type radiator and starting handle.

Norman Thompson had been taken ill in October with a nervous breakdown and went to Egypt to recuperate. He was away until June 1915 and during his absence Dr.White ran the Company with the help of Mr.Dodds, the Office Manager, and Mr.Rounthwaite, the Works Manager.

The first machine, No.1195, was delivered to Dover Air Station in January 1915. As Norman Thompson was still recuperating abroad, 1195 was flown to Dover by Eric Gordon England with Dr.White as passenger. It was the first seaplane to be seen there since the outbreak of war and cheering crowds turned out to see them arrive. It was wrecked in a heavy landing on 15 February 1915 and was returned to Bognor where it was fitted with a new and strengthened hull, known as the N.T.2A type. The remaining five machines of this batch were progressively withdrawn from service and fitted with the new hull.

The first layer of one-eighth inch mahogany planks was riveted to frames diagonally and faired in; then the hull was covered with fabric affixed by glue. Finally the outer layer of planking was attached with copper rivets, the planks running horizontally. The hull was then rubbed down and varnished. In those days an erecting shop was marked out in squares and a chargehand and his men built the machine by hand from start to finish in each square. Each team had craftsmen from all the various trades required. There were no jigs.

The modified machines had an additional pair of struts between the hull and the front end of the engine-bearers. The main petrol tank, which originally had rested on the floor of the hull, was found to pound and break its bearers when the boat

White & Thompson No.3 (N.T.2) Flying Boats under construction at Middleton-on-Sea

was moving at speed on the water. In the new hull the tank was slung by steel straps from the front and rear main spars of the lower-wing. A steel tube passed through the hull under the tank, forming a structural member. The ends of the tube were open to receive the stub-axles of wheels which could be fitted in position for launching the boats or for manoeuvring on land.

This improved version was further developed in the early Summer of 1915. The thickness of the hull was reduced, the upper portion of the foredeck was covered with transparent material and the two fins mounted on the top-wing were moved further outboard to a position immediately above the outer interplane struts.

Mr.J.C.C.Taylor wrote in his autobiography:

"During my stay at Bognor, Mr.Norman Thompson called me into his office one day and asked me to collect six men and proceed to Dover as quickly as possible. It was very secret and all he could say was that it concerned one of the W & T Curtiss type boats. I was to report to Commander A.W.Bigsworth, who commanded the R.N.A.S. Station there. We duly arrived on a Sunday morning and I immediately contacted the Commander.

After swearing me to secrecy, locking the door and making sure we should not be overheard, he explained that on the following Thursday there was to be a mass raid on Calais (sic!). They were sending over everything they could lay their hands on, including a White and Thompson boat which at

present was unserviceable.

I asked what was wrong with the boat and where it was, and was told it was at the bottom of Dover harbour, but was being raised that afternoon.

It was duly lifted out of the water and on to the quay, and moved into an old skating-rink nearby which served as a hangar. Within an hour we set to work.

We continued day and night, right through until Thursday morning, with little sleep or food, but the flying boat was completed and ready to take off with the rest that afternoon.

To appreciate the formidable task we were required to complete in so short a time, it should be realised that the engine - a Beardmore Austro-Daimler - had to be completely dismantled, cleaned, certain parts replaced, reassembled and tested. The wings and tail surfaces had to be opened up, dried, repaired and resealed, and the hull of the boat repaired.

I cannot ever remember feeling so tired, or so hungry; and when the job was finished, and the aircraft had flown off, we were far too tired to eat or sleep."

These machines took off water very well, but the crew was always soaked as the cockpits were open without any protection.

The first flight of the true N.T.2A type (No.3807) was on 22 June 1915 and the one hour official approval flight by Gordon England and E.M.Speakman took place on 6 July, when 67 knots

White & Thompson No.3 on the beach at Middleton. Note early Union Flag insignia on the rudder

was achieved at 1,350 r.p.m. On its third flight, serious engine trouble was experienced when an exhaust valve broke and a heavy landing was made.

Two machines were built, Nos.3807 and 3808, the first of which was fitted with a 120 h.p. Beardmore engine; the second machine was powered by a 150 h.p. Hispano-Suiza, although this may had been installed whilst in service with the R.N.A.S. Both could mount a Lewis gun on a pillar on the port side of the cockpit. 3808 was fitted with dual control.

The N.T.2s and N.T.2As were mainly used for anti-submarine patrols but 3807 was wrecked by the C.O. of Calshot whilst attempting to chase Zeppelin L31 on the night of 25/26 September 1916.

The longest surviving N.T.2 was 1199. This machine, whilst being piloted by Flight Lieutenant D.Murray in an attack on the Belgian coast, was hit by A.A. fire and had to make a forced landing in the Wester Scheldt. It was towed into Vlissingen harbour by a torpedo boat on 17 February 1915 and interned. The Beardmore engine was repaired with parts from another Beardmore taken from an interned R.E.5 and 1199 was restored to flying condition. It was purchased by the Dutch Government in August 1916 for £1,500 and was given the serial number G1. It remained in service with the Dutch Navy until at least the end of 1917.

For the N.T.2A prototype of the N.T.2B see Chapter 10.

Specification

Type:	W & T No.3 Flying Boat (N.T.2 and N.T.2A)
Date:	1915/1916
Seats:	Two
Power:	120 h.p. Beardmore (N.T.2)
	150 h.p. Hispano-Suiza (N.T.2A)
Length	27 ft.6 in.
Height:	c 10 ft.6 in.
Span, upper:	45 ft.0in.
lower:	34 ft.0 in.
Chord	5 ft.6 in.
Empty weight:	1,850 lbs
Loaded weight:	2,803 lbs

Performance (N.T.2A):

Climb to 500 ft	2 minutes
Climb to 1,000 ft	4 minutes
Climb to 9,000 ft	20 minutes
Petrol capacity:	45 gallons
Propeller:	Four-bladed
Armament:	One Lewis gun,
	light bombs (total 150 lbs)

N.T.2A 3807 at Calshot. Note Lewis gun on front cockpit

Production and Serial Numbers:

Nos.1195-1200   Contract C.P.60401/14
Nos.3807-3808   Contract C.P.45183/15

Cost: Nos.3807/8 £1,600 each

Service Histories:

No.1195   Fitted Lewis gun on port side of cockpit and modified bracing; deld to 1 Sqn RNAS Dover 7.2.15 by Gordon England; Mkrs repair by 11.3.15; fitted Type 2A hull during repairs; engine cut on take-off; forcelanded by FSL C N Leeston Smith and damaged tailplane strut 29.6.15; engine cut and forcelanded in rough sea and badly damaged by PFSL T V Lister and PO Boyd; for survey 2.7.15; tested after repair 31.7.15; Dunkerque 16.9.15; Dover 8.10.15; Calshot flying school 8.10.15 to at least 6.18; deleted 11.7.18

No.1196   Deld Fort George by 28.2.15; ready for test 6.3.15; ready for examination by Admiralty Overseer 30.3.15; erected at Dundee 12.11.15; deleted 7.1.16

No.1197   Deld to 1 Sqn RNAS at Dover 9.2.15 and bows damaged by Lt Whitehouse on arrival; prop damaged 11.2.15; tested 26.2.15; remained at Dover when 1 Sqn moved to France; with Defence Flight by 1.4.15; flown by Flt Cdr S D A Grey on hostile seaplane patrol 20.3.15; damaged on landing 11.4.15; dismantled 5.15; probably fitted with new hull 5.15; tested 30.7.15; flown on anti-Zeppelin patrol by FSL T V Lister and LM McSorley, 19.8.15; Dunkerque 12.10.15; Dover 4.11.15; Bembridge 6.11.15; Deleted 24.10.16

No.1198   Allotted to Fort George by 11.3.15 but crashed on landing 22.2.15; still at Bognor 12.3.15; probably fitted with new hull; deld to Dover 14.9.15; Calshot 17.12.15; Deleted 24.10.16

No.1199   Deld to 1 Sqn RNAS Dover 11.2.15; with 1 Sqn in France 14.2.15; hit by AA over Flanders and force-landed in Wester Scheldt near Vlissingen, 17.2.15; interned and impressed in R.Neth Navy as G1; crashed 17.7.16; at Schellingwoude 21.8.17; at De Mok 1.11.17

No.1200   Deld to Fort George 27.3.15 for erection; tested 15.4.15; wrecked by FSL Gamwell on landing off Chanonry Point 1.5.15; remains to Bognor; deleted 5.15

No.1198 on the beach at Middleton

No.3807   Deld to Calshot but crashed on collection from Bognor at Havant, 16.9.15; modified engine bearers and forward-firing Lewis gun; Bognor for trials 10.15; Calshot 3.11.15; damaged by Flt Cdr Kershaw and Sub Lt Gregory 19.11.15; engine failed on anti-Zeppelin patrol by Sqn Cdr A W Bigsworth; forcelanded and slightly damaged, 25/26.9.16; Calshot for training by 2.17; deletion recommended 6.6.17 as beyond repair; deleted 11.7.17.

No.3808   Fitted with dual control; deld Calshot 12.10.15; training at Calshot by 2.17; deleted 27.4.17

White & Thompson No.3 completed at Middleton

No.1199 interned in the Netherlands. Note Dutch insignia on rudder

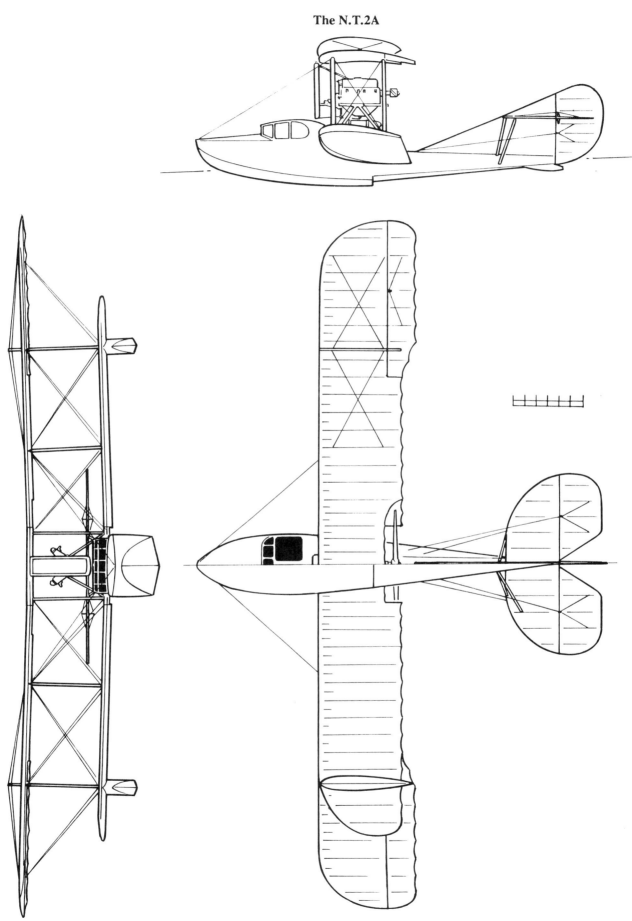

The N.T.2A

The N.T.3 "Bognor Bloater" on the cliff edge at Middleton

CHAPTER 7

The N.T.3 "Bognor Bloater" Biplane

The outbreak of war in August 1914 found Britain woefully short of military aircraft and both the War Office and the Admiralty engaged in a hectic scramble to impress whatever civilian machines were available, however unsuitable they might be. The Admiralty had already laid plans to standardise on one of the few successful pre-war designs, the Royal Aircraft Factory B.E.2c biplane and they invited the majority of the established aircraft manufacturers in the country to quote for the supply of batches of this machine. Vickers and Blackburn were offered contracts for 36 each, Beardmore and Grahame-White 24 each, Hewlett and Blondeau 18, Martinsyde 12 and Eastbourne Aviation Company 6. Surprisingly, White and Thompson, with little experience of building landplanes, were invited to quote for 12 B.E.2cs.

However, Norman Thompson and his recently appointed chief designer Percy Beadle decided that they could improve on the B.E.2c design and submitted their plans to the Admiralty. They were promptly given a contract for twelve machines, which were known as the N.T.3.

The flight organs were similar to those of the B.E.2c, but its outstanding and novel feature was its light wooden boat-built body which, for only a slight increase in weight, gave the following advantages compared with the usual type of wire-braced, fabric-covered fuselage:

(1) A simple, well-established method of constructing the body and the best-known streamline form with minimum head resistance.

(2) A permanently rigid structure which obviated the use of wire-bracing and periodic truing-up.

(3) Greater strength and protection to the crew, in the event of a crash, due to local crushing of the wooden skin and absence of wooden spars liable to snap and form lethal splinters.

Designed in September 1914, this was probably one of, if not the first true monocoque fuselages built. The work was entrusted to the boat builders H.Williams of Littlehampton, who had previously built the hull of the No.1 Flying Boat. The internal structure consisted of formers and stringers over which Consuta copper-stitched cedar plywood was diagonally applied, giving an exterior surface which was remarkably free from undulations and local

N.T.3 fuselages under construction at H Williams & Co., Littlehampton

buckling. It was then varnished and polished in true boat-builder style. The completed fuselages were taken by road to Middleton, where they were then mated to the wings, tail assembly and undercarriages and the 70 h.p. Renault engines were installed.

It has been suggested that a crude brake, in the form of a claw, was attached to the undercarriage and when released dug into the ground. However, no trace of this installation is visible in any of the photographs which have been found.

The first machine, No.1171, was rolled out at the beginning of March 1915 and the first flight was made on 8 March with Gordon England at the controls. It was also flown by Clifford Prodger and Commander John Seddon, chief test pilot to the Admiralty, who both reported most favourably on the N.T.3. It was found to be 2 m.p.h. faster than the standard B.E.2c.

Unfortunately, the 70 h.p. Renault engines do not seem to have been as reliable as the airframes and at least two test flights were marred by engine failure. Gordon England was flying one day in quite a stiff wind when a cylinder cracked and the engine came to an abrupt halt. The pilot had to make a sharp turn over the sea to land on the sands. Unfortunately there was not sufficient room to spare and the machine alighted in about two feet of water. This checked its landing run so sharply that it turned over on the tips of its skids, balanced for a few seconds with its tail in the air, and toppled right over on its back, remaining balanced on the upper

wing and the rudder post. The pilot then unstrapped his safety belt, turned a slow somersault round the control wheel and dropped to the ground. He escaped merely with wet feet. On examination it was found that the only real damage was a broken propeller and broken skid-tips and some water-deterioration of the top wing. The fuselage was complete undamaged.

On another occasion, a forced landing was made due to engine failure and both the Admiralty test pilot and Lieutenant Speakman, the resident inspector at that time, who were in the machine, attributed the fact that they got off with their lives and without a scratch, entirely to the manner in which the body was built.

No.1171 was accepted by the Admiralty in July 1915 after sand tests on the wings had proved satisfactory. It would appear that, of the twelve machines built, ten were erected and flown and the remaining two were used for spares. The order was completed in September 1915 and the N.T.3s were used at Eastchurch, Eastbourne, Yarmouth, Grain, Chingford and Hendon. Their main function was the training of pilots but those at the coastal air stations were also used for patrol duties.

The R.N.A.S. nicknamed this machine the *Bognor Bloater* in reference to its place of origin, the bloater-like shape of the body and the suggestion of scales created by the copper stitching of the plywood fuselage.

The N.T.3 seems to have had a short life in active service but was quite popular, being fast and

N.T.3s in service with the Royal Naval Air Service at Eastbourne

stable. The strong fuselage inspired confidence in the pilot and passenger and no doubt if it had been used in a more war-like role, it would have stood up to a considerable amount of punishment.

SPECIFICATION

Type:	Norman Thompson N.T.3 Biplane
Date:	1914/16
Seats:	Two
Power:	70 H.P. Renault
Length:	c 28 ft. 3 in.
Height:	c 12 ft. 0 in.
Span (upper):	c 37 ft. 0 in.
(lower)	c 32 ft. 6 in.
Chord:	c 6 ft. 0 in.
Tail span:	c 12 ft. 0 in.
Tail chord:	c 7 ft. 6 in.
Propeller	c 10 ft. 4 in. four-bladed
Armament	Probably nil

No.1171 at Middleton

Production

12 aircraft   Nos.1171 - 1182

Service Histories:

No.1171   First flight at Bognor 8.3.15; ready for delivery at Bognor 30.4.15; Bognor under repair by 31.5.15; tested 25.6.15; deld to 2 Sqn RNAS Eastchurch (via Eastbourne) 25.6.15; Eastchurch flying school 27.6.15; wrecked 30.6.15; deleted 9.7.15

No.1172   Deld to 2 Sqn RNAS Eastchurch 30.4.15; Eastchurch flying school 27.6.15; dismantled 13.10.15; surveyed and to CSD White City 22.11.15

No.1173   Tested at Bognor 22.4.15; deld Eastbourne flying school 27.6.15; dis-mantled 5.10.15; deleted 10.12.15

No.1174   Deld to Killingholme 11.5.15; tested 15.5.15; retd Bognor; retd Killingholme and tested after alterations by Gordon England 4.6.15; Chingford for erection 8.6.154; Hendon 21.6.15; deleted 31.7.15

No.1175   Tested at Bognor 5.5.15; Eastbourne flying school 21.6.15; dismantled by 1.10.15; deleted 10.12.15

No.1176   Deld to Yarmouth by road 26.6.15; tested 2.7.15 by Gordon England; damaged chassis on landing by Sub Lt Hilliard and AM Williams 12.7.15; engine removed 14.7.15; under repair Yarmouth 16.7.15 and still there on 31.8.15; no further trace

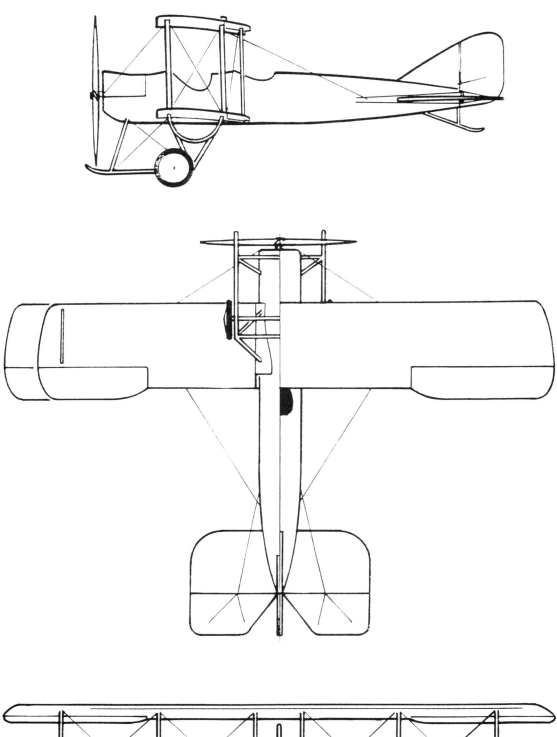

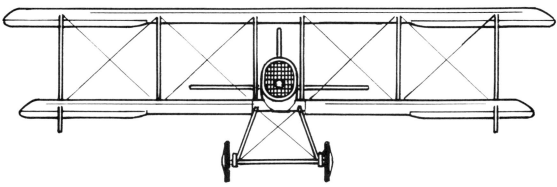

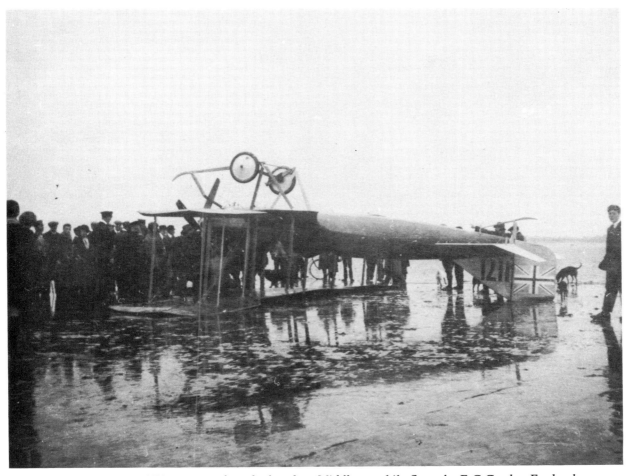

1171 overturned on the beach at Middleton while flown by E C Gordon England

No.1177   Deld to Yarmouth by rail 12.8.15; acceptance test by 7.9.15 and rejected as "out of true"; to Killingholme, awaiting further acceptance test 16.9.15 to 2.10.15; to Yarmouth, awaiting acceptance 16.11.15; accepted 19.12.15 by Pickles; to CSD White City 4.1.16 (arrived 10.1.16); to Survey Dept 17.1.16

No.1178   Bognor by 31.8.15; Killingholme awaiting acceptance 16.9.15; not accepted; Bognor for trials by 31.10.15; to CSD White City 14.2.16

No.1179   Deld to Grain by road 28.9.15 (not accepted); Bognor by 31.10.15; Kingsnorth by 31.3.16; deleted 4.16

No.1180   Bognor by 31.8.15; only accepted as spares

No.1181   Only accepted for spares 14.9.15

No.1182   Only accepted for spares 14.9.15

1171 being prepared for flight at Middleton

N.T.4 8339 on its beaching trolley with experimental shell-firing gun and large radio aerial mast

CHAPTER 8

The N.T.4, N.T.4a and N.2C "Small America" Flying Boats

Although the twin-engined "Circuit of Britain" Flying Boat had not been particularly successful, Percy Beadle had worked on the hull design to make certain improvements and, when in June 1915 Norman Thompson returned to work full of enthusiasm to expand the business, between them they produced plans for an enlarged twin-engined machine. The design looked so promising that the Company was given an Admiralty order for six examples in July 1915; the tender price being finally accepted on 28 December 1915. Since 21 September, the Company had been renamed The Norman Thompson Flight Company and the new machine was given the type number N.T.4.

The existing buildings were inadequate for increased production and Dr.White felt that a move should be made to a totally new location with more space and a more sheltered site for testing flying boats. Norman Thompson disagreed and insisted that the expansion should be at Middleton. By then Dr.White felt that he could be of more use to the country as a doctor and therefore left to join the Royal Army Medical Corps. His interest in the firm was bought out by Norman Thompson's father. The

new sheds were then built.

The original "Circuit of Britain" machine had been allocated the serial number 883; the serial 1267 was allocated to a White & Thompson flying boat with two 90 h.p. Curtiss engines. This may had been the "missing link" between the Circuit flying boat and the N.T.4 and this would tie in with a Company statement that the Admiralty supplied a pair of 90 h.p. Curtiss engines. However, this machine never apparently materialised in this form and the number 1267 was re-allocated to the Pemberton-Billing P.B.9, the "Seven Day Bus".

The N.T.4 was a large and handsome flying boat, similar in layout to the Curtiss H.4. Although both the Curtiss H.4 and the N.T.4 were known as "Small Americas", they differed quite considerably in detail design. The N.T.4 was bigger, with four-bay wings and pusher engines and hull design owed more to Percy Beadle than to Porte/Curtiss.

The single-stepped hull, built by Williams of Littlehampton, had keel and frames of elm with ash chines and stringers and formers of spruce. One skin of mahogany ply was applied diagonally with copper rivets, a layer of calico was then glued on

The N.T.4 prototype No.8338 on the slip at Middleton with two 100 hp Green engines

overall and a final layer of ply planks was then riveted on horizontally. The fins of the hull, running forward from the step, were attached separately after completion of the remainder of the hull. Buoyancy of the hull was achieved by means of fabric bulkheads aft of the crew compartment. A fully glazed enclosed cockpit was provided; this and the bows of the hull were progressively modified, the prototype having a blunt nose.

The four-bay wings were of unequal span and the top wing extensions were braced to triangular king-posts above the outer interplane struts. The lower wing of the prototype was of 3 ft.5 in. greater span than that of subsequent machines. The first batch produced had broad chord ailerons projecting beyond the wing trailing-edge; subsequent batches had the normal constant chord ailerons. Wings, tailplane, fin and rudder were all fabric covered, but some later machines had the bottom of the rudder ply-covered as the N.T.4 was an inveterate "tail-dragger".

The engines were mounted on bearers attached to fore and aft pairs of ash struts, these being cross-braced to the central interplane struts by metal tubes and strops. The N.T.4 was originally designed to be powered by two 100 h.p. Green pusher engines. However, it was soon realised that these would give inadequate power and only 8338 was so fitted. In June 1916, the Admiralty Air Department invest-igated the probable performance and recommended that a trial installation of 140 h.p. Hispano-Suizas should be made and on 22 July Norman Thompsons

were invited to tender for fitting 140 h.p. Hispanos in 8338-8343 and 9061-9064. The Air Department also advised Norman Thompson on the design of pusher propellers for the Hispano. The entire centre-section, interplane struts and engine bearers had to be redesigned by Mr.A.Bedford, the chief draughtsman, to allow for the installation of the 8-cylinder V type 150 h.p. Hispano-Suiza in place of the 6-cylinder vertical Green. 8338 was re-engined and the remainder of the batch had the 150 h.p. Hispano fitted. The second batch 9061-9064 initially had this engine but 9063 and 9064 were sub-sequently fitted with 200 h.p. Hispanos.

The delays caused by the engine change meant that it was 27 October before 8338 was ready for trials and by then all fitting, wings and tailplanes were complete for the remaining nine machines and they could have been delivered quickly if the trials had been satisfactory.

The first machines do not seem to have had gravity fuel tanks, but later on they were fitted with a small tank under the top wing above each engine. The engines were totally uncowled and a large vertical radiator was attached to the top half of the interplane struts in front of each engine. A starting handle protruded from the radiator.

Normal armament consisted of a Lewis gun mounted on the roof of the cockpit and two 230 lb. (or a combination of 65 lb. and 16 lb.) bombs on racks under the lower wing. In April 1916, 8338 was experimentally fitted with a 2-pounder Davis gun on a parallel sliding mounting above the cabin

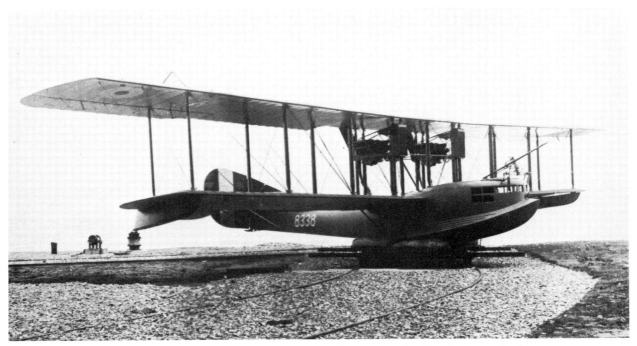

No.8338 with an experimental installation of a two-pounder Davis gun in the bows

roof and 8339 had a Vickers Q.F. gun in the same place on a substantial tubular mount. As this large machine had a crew of only two, the second pilot/navigator also had to act as gunner. 9063 was experimentally fitted with a Type 52B W/T set.

Nos.8339 - 8341 were delivered in January 1917. 8342/8343 and 9061/9062 followed in February and March. 9063/9064 were not completed until June 1917. Prior to delivery, the prows of 8338/8339 and 9061 - 9064 were altered to improve their take-off characteristics and were despatched to Killingholme to await arrival of their Hispano engines and starting gear.

Mr.George Sims, a chargehand in the Erecting Shop, wrote:

"In 1913 I joined an aircraft firm, the White and Thompson Company. My first job was to help build Curtiss flying boats. Then came the 400 h.p. twin motor flying-boats with enclosed cabin. We used to pump the fuel up to a gravity tank for take-off and then a pump driven by a small outside propeller took over the job. I used to fly in these boats with Clifford Prodger. The first time I flew with him he asked me to get him a piece of iron rod about twelve inches long and three-quarters of an inch diameter and a good pair of cutting pliers. I asked him why he wanted these and he told me that the rod was to crack anyone who looked like touching the controls, which were dual, and the pliers to cut his way out of a crash, as in these machines there were flying cables, landing cables, incidence cables, drift cables, etc., in fact a maze of wires. In my next trial flight with him we crashed in

the Moray Firth; the cause was a cracked cylinder in a motor. His pliers got us out of the aircraft and we were fished out of the water with boat-hooks from a motor launch."

No.8340 was test flown at Dundee on 15 May 1918 by Flight Lieutenant N.H.Woodhead and was experimentally fitted with "large fins". These improved the take-off performance but made the machine tail heavy in flight. Professor Sir Austin Robinson comments on this as follows:

"My own guess is that they (i.e. R.N.A.S. Dundee) tried to take 8340 seriously as a potential patrol boat and found that she was very difficult to get off with a full load. The weight figures give a loaded weight of 6,469 lbs (empty weight 4,572 lbs) which loaded is 21.5 lbs per h.p. on 300 h.p. In the ordinary way we did not load a N.T.4 much over 5,500 lbs - about 18 lbs per h.p. for school work. In that case it made sense to see whether it was possible to enlarge the fins of the hull, projecting outside the hull itself, to increase the beam of the flotation and hydroplaning bottom (an F boat usually had "DO NOT WALK ON THE FINS" painted on it).

It would be a major job but old R.N.A.S. "Chippies" were very skilled and experienced and they may have tried to do it. If this was what they did it makes sense of "improved take-off". If the increase of beam was largely in the neighbourhood of the step, the C.G. might have been moved aft. But this is only a guess."

N.T.4a N2147 taken on 11 February 1918 at Middleton

A later version, the N.T.4a, had a slightly modified hull, 200 h.p. Hispano engines with enlarged radiators and a large gravity tank centrally mounted above the top wing. Two-bladed pusher propellers were fitted, both rotating in the same direction.

The completion of the first N.T.4s had been so delayed by the lack of a suitable engine and by various changes in Admiralty policy that, by the time they entered service, the Curtiss H.12s and Felixstowe F.2as, with much greater range, were being used for long-distance anti-submarine patrols. The N.T.4s were therefore mainly used for training crews at Killingholme and Calshot as replacement for the aging H.4s. However, 8339 and 8340 were based at Dundee and carried out patrols over the North Sea. Sir Austin Robinson is sceptical that N.T.4s or N.T.4as were ever used for long-distance patrols and he comments:

"My first trip in a N.T.4 was with four people aboard. I was only a passenger. There were two Killingholme school instructors, myself and another second pilot (Massey). My log-book says "Machine only got off once when Flight Commander Davies flew her. No control".

My second trip was also in 8343 with Massey flying with two of us aboard. My log-book says "Massey flying. Machine out of truth, particularly rudder". My third trip, three aboard, myself not flying. "Did not get off. Lost starboard propeller. Water in port carburettor, so towed in".

My fourth trip, in 8343. Self and two other second pilots. Self flying. "First solo (on N.T.4).

Wonderful bump over tanker (Naval oil reserve)."

Five or six weeks later, before taking 9062 to Lee-on-Solent. Self and Air Mechanic. "Machine test. Very tail heavy. Could not proceed to Felixstowe".

My own scepticism is greatly reinforced by actual experience of trying to fly one in the sort of conditions that would have been necessary for a patrol of 3-4 hours rather than the 20-minute hops required on school work. When the Killingholme school flight was transferred to Lee-on-Solent in order to make room for the Americans to accommodate the 50 H.16s that they brought with them, it became necessary to get 9062 to Lee-on-Solent. Since I lived at Winchester and saw the possibility of a week-end at home, I rashly volunteered to fly it down and, after a test trip and some re-rigging, I started out with a competent mechanic and a (so-called) second pilot who could neither fly nor navigate.

We struggled down the Lincolnshire and Norfolk coasts, nearly running into a Yarmouth Short because of the lack of visibility from the cabin of the N.T.4, We ultimately reached Felixstowe, despite increasing signs of overheating. We found when we arrived that the water had almost boiled away, the fabric covering of the props had been charred by the exhaust and the engine starting gear broke when we tried to restart the engines. I had had enough of ferrying N.T.4s and my mechanic and I returned sadly home, leaving the "second pilot" to find his way to Lee. But nothing short of very solid evidence will make me believe that N.T.4s did the sort of slogging patrol work that we

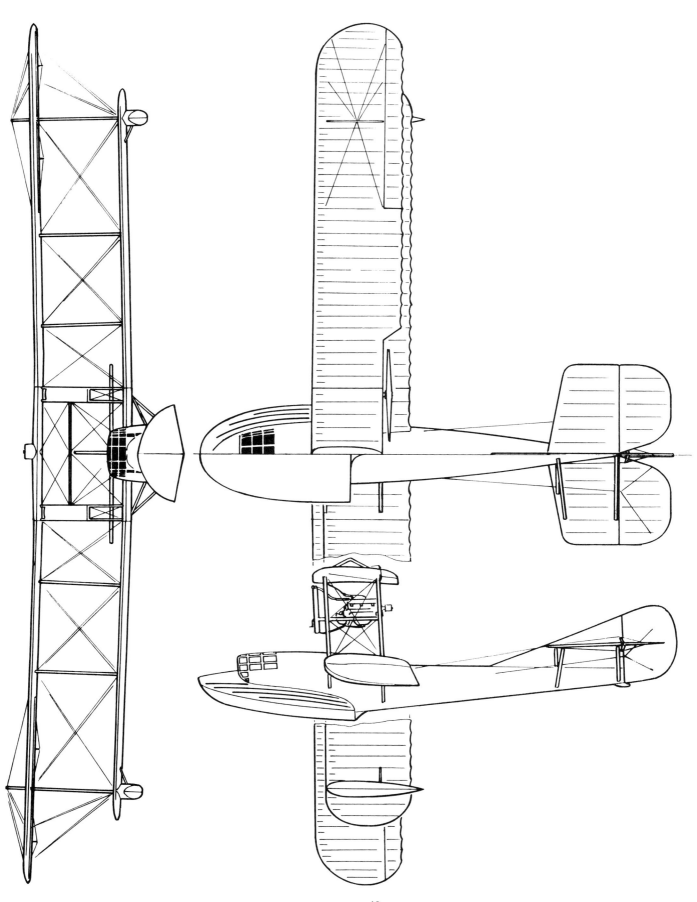

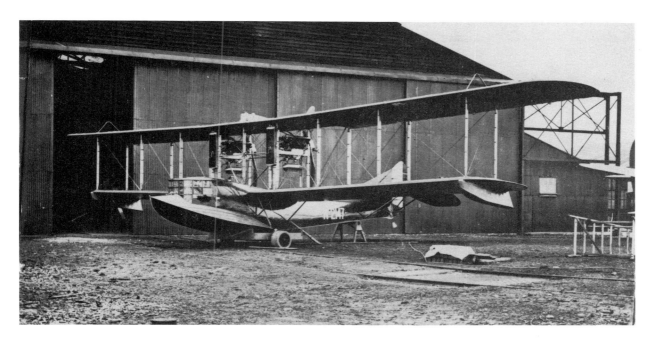

N.T.4a N2147 completed outside the main hangar at Middleton

did with Short 184s and Curtiss H.12s. I have not found any such evidence.

The N.T.4s were notoriously tail-heavy and the Centre of Gravity was not where it was supposed to be. If one were landing an N.T.4 one had to keep its tail up. If the water was not dead flat as one tried to land, a wave hit the tail first, bumped it up and one then hit a wave with the main step at above stalling speed and one bounced. On take-off, the N.T.4s were congenital tail-draggers with a bad take-off and a bad landing performance. "

Twenty N.T.4s (Nos. N2140 - N2159) were ordered in May 1917 and N2140 was delivered on 1 July. Deliveries continued during 1917 and 1918 and the final machine of the batch was not completed until June 1918. Suddenly, on 25 January 1918, the Air Board ordered all work on the N.T.4a to be suspended following a change of policy on the type of aircraft to be used for anti-submarine patrols. However, with timber already cut and most of the fittings fabricated, Thompsons were allowed to carry on with the completion of the batch N2140 - N2159. Some of this batch was delivered to units but the majority went straight to store and eventually on to the books of the Aircraft Disposal Board. One to the Civil Register as G-EAOY.

The following extracts from the log book of Lieutenant Maurice Fairhurst of R.N. Seaplane Station, Scilly Islands, gives a graphic illustration of some of the difficulties involved in flying the N.T.4A:

26.11.17	N2141	Delivery from Norman Thompson Flight Co. at Bognor. Konked (sic)
		at St.Catherines Point. Towed Calshot.
14.12.17	N2141	Left Calshot. Konked (sic) and towed to Poole, however, starboard plane washed away by heavy seas.
2.1.18	N2141	Poole to Portland
4.1.18	N2141	Got off and could only just manage to force nose down to descend. Found 20 gals water in tail.
7.1.18	N2141	Portland to Cattewater. Ran through snow twice. Wind all round the compass.
13.3.18	N2146	Bognor to Cowes
18.3.18	N2146	Cowes to Brixham. Landed owing to leaking radiator.
20.3.18	N2146	Torquay to Cattewater

The total remaining stock was sold by the Board to the Aircraft Disposal Company (a subsidiary of Handley Page) and on 6 December 1920, all the remaining N.T.4as were ordered to be scrapped.

A contract for a further batch of twenty (N2740 - N2759), placed in late 1917, was suspended on 7 February 1918 and cancelled on 1 June 1918.

As is related in Chapter 14, the expansion of the Middleton Works had been largely to cater for the extra space required for the construction of the N.T.4a and the raising of the necessary finance to pay for the new buildings and equipment was to lead eventually to the collapse of the Company.

In August 1917, Norman Thompson were invited to tender for the production of two prototypes of a

N.T.4as under construction at Middleton

N.T.4a N2151 on its beaching trolley

revised version of the N.T.4a to the N.2c specification. This was to combine the wings and tail unit of the N.T.4a with a hull constructed on the Porte/Felixstowe principle instead of the boat-built hulls normally fitted. Hulls for the Felixstowe F.2A boats had been built at Littlehampton for several months and Thompsons had little difficulty in designing a suitable hull for the N.T.4a replacement.

The original specification called for two 200 h.p. Hispanos. Norman Thompson did not anticipate that this installation would attain the required performance and proposed a similar design but with three 200 h.p. Hispanos instead. However, the Admiralty insisted on a twin-engined machine and a design was therefore submitted with two 200 h.p. Sunbeam Arabs.

Thompson's tender of £3.600 for individual machines, or £3,400 each for quantity production, was accepted by the Admiralty and Contract AS.33477 (BR 237) for two prototypes was awarded on 23 November 1917.

Drawings of the new hull were completed by early in 1918 and construction commenced in January. The hull was a plywood-covered, cross-braced wooden girder structure with a stern-post shorter than on the N.T.4a. The twin 200 h.p. Sunbeam Arab engines were installed as pushers and had four-bladed propellers.

The first hull was transferred from Littlehampton to the erecting shops at Middleton in April 1918 and the basic structure was virtually complete and awaiting delivery of its Sunbeam engines by mid-June. The engines were installed and the centre-section completed by 26 June; the tail and fin had been erected and rigging was under way. The second machine was well ahead of schedule and was awaiting arrival of its engines.

The first machine, N82, had its initial trials on 1 August when it was found that the tail suction of the hull was too great and the machine rose to past its stalling angle before leaving the water. It was returned to the workshops for modification. Progress with the second machine, N83, was slowed down to await the results on N82. In an effort to improve the take-off characteristics, the rear step of the hull was deepened. By now the N.2c, as the new machine was called, was found to be 600 lbs overweight on the design estimates; the hull, alone being 200 lbs overweight.

Work on N82 was still held up at the beginning of October pending delivery of some channel iron to be used to stiffen the engine bearers and N83 was at an advanced stage awaiting the trials of N82.

On 16 October, N82 was flown by a Naval Air Section test pilot who found that it handled better but porpoised badly at 30 knots and was very tail heavy in the air.

By mid-November, the N.2c's future was in doubt and work was in abeyance pending suggestions from the firm of improvements to be incorporated. By now the war was over and the peace-time cut-backs had started. On 31 December, the Air Ministry recommended that the two machines be deleted - N83 was, in fact, never completed. By now the boat-builders at Littlehampton were filling in their time constructing dinghies.

There are shadowy documentary references to a N.T.4b Flying Boat. It seems likely that this was the Norman Thompson number given to the N.2c.

N.T.4 No.8343 at Killingholme seaplane station

Specification

Type:	N.T.4 and N.T.4a Flying Boat
Date:	1916-1918
Seats:	Two
Power:	Two 100 h.p. Green (8338 only)
	Two 150 h.p. Hispano-Suiza
	(8338-8345; 9061-9064)
	Two 200 h.p. Hispano-Suiza
	(9063-9064; N2140-N2159)
	Two 200 h.p. Sunbeam Arab (N82/83)

Dimensions:

	N.T.4 Prototype	N.T.4 Production	N.T.4a Production
Span: upper	78 ft.0 in.	77 ft.10 in.	78 ft.7 in.
lower	64 ft.3 in.	64 ft.3 in.	60 ft.10 in.
Chord:	7 ft.6 in.	7 ft.6 in.	7 ft.6 in.
Gap:	7 ft.6 in.	7 ft.6 in.	7 ft.6 in.
Stagger:	Nil		8½ in.
Dihedral:		1 deg 30 min	
Incidence:		5 degrees	
Tailplane span:	16 ft.9 in.		16 ft.0 in.
Tailplane chord:	11 ft.0 in.		
Length:	39 ft.9 in.	40 ft.9 in.	41 ft.6 in.
Height:	15 ft.0 in.	14 ft.7 in.	14 ft.10 in.
Wing area:		1,014 sq ft	997.8 sq ft
Tailplane area:			136.5 sq ft
Fin and rudder area:			55.9 sq ft
Weight empty:			4,572 lbs
Weight loaded:			6,469 lbs
		N.2c	6,193.5 lbs

Performance:

	N.T.4	N.T.4a
Max speed at 2,000 ft	96 m.p.h.	95 m.p.h.
Max speed at 6,500 ft	93 m.p.h.	93 m.p.h.
Max speed at 10,000 ft	90 m.p.h.	91 m.p.h.
Climb to 2,000 ft	3 min 30 sec	3 min 50 sec
Climb to 6,500 ft	12 min 30 sec	15 min
Climb to 10,000 ft 25 min	31 min 5 sec	
Max ceiling:	14,500 ft	14,000 ft
Endurance:	4½ hours flat out	
	6 hours at 60 kts	

Armament: 1 Lewis gun. 16-lb or 65-lb bombs or two 230-lb bombs

Wireless:	Type 52B
Cost:	£3,250 plus £46 for trolley

Control column and instruments on an N.T.4a

N.2c at Middleton with some of the work force. Note Sunbeam Arab engines and four-bladed propellers

Production and Serial Numbers:

8338-8343	6 N.T.4	Contract C.P.145936/15
9061-9064	4 N.T.4	Contract C.P.145936/15
N82-N83	2 N.2c	Contract A.D. Spec. N.2(c)
N2140-2159	20 N.T.4a	Contract A.S.12528 (B.R.63) 16 completed
N2740-2759	20 N.T.4a	Contract A.S.32477 (B.R.225). Cancelled

Service History

8338　On trial at Bognor 20.10.16 - 15.12.16; experimental Davis 2-pounder gun in nose; Calshot 5.4.17; Calshot School by 10.17 - 2.11.17; deleted 8.11.17

8339　Erected 15.12.16; fitted to carry two 230-lb bombs for anti-sub patrols; erected at Killingholme 15.1.17; to Dundee by lorry 29.4.17; deletion by 25.5.18

8340　Fitted to carry two 230-lb bombs; to Killingholme 15.1.17; to Dundee by lorry 29.4.17; damaged by 6.10.17; large fins fitted; tested 15.5.18; deleted 18.7.18

8341　Fitted to carry two 230-lb bombs; to Killingholme 15.1.17; deleted 8.1.18 as total loss

8342　(150 hp); fitted to carry two 230 lb bombs; deld to Killingholme Seaplane School for erection 22.3.17; in storage by 19.1.18; deleted 3.5.18

8343　(150 hp); fitted to carry two 230-lb bombs; deld to Killingholme Seaplane School for erection 22.3.17; 6.10.17; in storage by 19.1.18; to reserve 5.18; deleted 3.5.18

9061　Calshot School by 10.17 to 2.11.17; deleted 6.11.17 as wrecked

9062　Deld to Killingholme store by 16.4.17; Killingholme School by 27.4.18; Felixstowe 8.5.18; to Felixstowe School by 25.5.18 to 25.7.18; deleted 5.9.18

9063　Delivered 23.6.17; to Grain Test Depot 14.7.17 for experiments with Type 52B Wireless Transmitter; to Westgate but sprang a leak, moored to buoy and sank; wreck towed ashore 7.1.18; SOC 11.1.18 and deleted 17.1.18

9064　Delivered 21.6.17; to Westgate 3.9.17; to Calshot en route to Killingholme 12.9.17; hull and wings damaged in bad weather at Westgate 13.9.17; mkrs by 3.18 for repair; expected for trials after repair by mkrs. 6.4.18; possibly used in Victory Celebrations at Littlehampton

N82　First flight 1.8.18; first tested by Naval Air Section pilot 16.10.18; allotment to Grain cancelled by 14.11.18; deleted 31.12.18

N83　Built but not erected; deleted 31.12.18

N2140　Delivered to Calshot by 7.12.17; Cattewater by 28.12.17; deleted 27.6.18

N2141　Delivered to Calshot 26.11.17; Cattewater by 14.12.17; deleted 27.6.18

N2142　Delivered to Calshot by 9.11.17; at Calshot School January 1918; for Killingholme 19.1.18

N2143　Delivered to Calshot by 16.11.17; for Killingholme 19.1.18

N2144　Delivered to Calshot School 11.17; for Killingholme by 19.1.18

N.T.4a in service with the Royal Naval Air Service

N2145	Delivered 15.12.17; allocated to S.W. Group by 30.3.18 but deleted at Mkrs 9.5.18
N2146	Delivered to Cattewater 20.3.18 to 5.18; deleted 27.6.18
N2147	Delivered 19.1.18; Portland by 4.18; Cattewater 5.4.18 to 5.18; deleted 27.6.18
N2148	Delivered 2.2.18; Calshot by 30.3.18 for Cattewater; deleted 24.4.18
N2149	Delivered to Newhaven by 30.3.18; MAD Grain 27.4.18 to 29.8.18; deleted 26.9.18
N2150	Delivered 30.3.18 to Killingholme Seaplane School; Felixstowe School 9.5.18; deleted 29.8.18
N2151	Delivered 20.4.18 to Westgate; Felixstowe Seaplane School 5.18 to 7.18; deleted 29.8.18
N2152	Delivered 4.5.18; for Killingholme
N2153	Delivered 11.5.18
N2154	Delivered 18.5.18
N2155	Delivered 25.5.18; regd 29.10.19 and became G-EAOY; cancelled 10.20

N2156 to N2158; probably never completed
N2740 to N2759; Contract cancelled 1.6.18

The first hull of the second batch of N.T.4s just completed by H Williams & Co at Littlehampton

N.T.5 N1059 at Calshot

CHAPTER 9

The N.T.5 - The Modified F.B.A.Model B Flying Boat

The Franco-British Aviation Company Ltd was formed in November 1913 to take over the two French builders of waterplanes - H.Levêque and Société Tellier. The directors of the new company were Reginald Mortimer, Captain A.W.Gamlen, Engineer-Captain A.R.Rolle and Lieutenant-Colonel E.J.de Salis. The managers were Captain André Beaumont and Louis Schreck. The company held a licence to build and sell Curtiss flying boats in France and to sell them in other parts of the world with the exception of Britain, Russia, Italy and the U.S.A.

The company had been founded with patriotic as well as purely commercial motives, to handle the very best aircraft and engines available so as to bring Britain into the forefront of World aviation. The experience of Levêque, Tellier and Schreck with waterplanes meant that the company's first products were small flying boats designed by Levêque and sold to the Austro-Hungarian, Swedish and Danish navies and known as F.B.A.-Levêque. Subsequent machines were designed by Schreck and were known simply as F.B.A.

The Model A with a 100 h.p. Gnôme engine was followed in 1915 by the Model B with a 100 h.p. Gnôme Monosoupape driving a pusher propeller. The Model B was ordered by the French Navy and the R.N.A.S. who bought forty of the French-built machines, initially for coastal patrols and later for training.

Whilst it was quite a well-designed machine, with a lively performance, it was not really strong enough for open-sea work and the rigours of "circuits and bumps" and many hulls were badly damaged in heavy landings.

In July 1916, Norman Thompson were asked to design a strengthened hull for the F.B.A. and were invited to tender for the supply of twenty machines of a completely revised version. The new hull was married to new wings which were slightly swept back and the tailplane was set at a negative angle of incidence. The changes were so major that the company allotted its own type number N.T.5 to the new design. At the same time they were given a contract to build and fit new hulls to four damaged F.B.A. boats (Nos.3201, 3206, 9607 and 9608). Their initial tender prices for a batch of twenty were found to be too high and they were asked to revise

Norman Thompson N.T.5 prototype, the modified F.B.A. Model B . Note the original flat-topped rear hull

them. Work commenced in the Autumn and, by the end of October 1916, the first machine, N1040, was being erected and delivery of its engine was awaited. Strangely, whilst all the others of the batch had the rear hull section in the form of a triangle with the apex uppermost, N1040 had the hull section "inverted". By then the hulls of the next four were under construction and Norman Thompson said that they could build six more simultaneously if skilled labour was obtainable. Six sets of wings and tail fittings had been completed.

The first of the reconstructed F.B.A.s (9601) was finished by 7 November; its trials were completed by 9 December and it was delivered to Calshot on 15 December. 9608 had been held up owing to alteration of its wings.

The hulls of N1040-N1049 were almost ready by mid-November and N1051 and N1052 were well in hand. By the end of January 1918, N1040 was nearly ready for trials and the remainder of the batch was due to follow at about five per month; however, some snag was discovered and the whole batch was held up for alterations until March.

Norman Thompson received a further order for ten N.T.5 hulls in the Summer of 1917 and it is assumed that these were fitted as replacements to some of the French-built F.B.A.s.

Percy Beadle left Norman Thompson on 31 December 1917 and went as General Manager and Chief Designer to Gosport Aviation and no doubt the sixty F.B.A.s built by them incorporated the improvements which had been introduced by

Norman Thompson.

The hazards of flying boat primary training led to many accidents and, by March 1918, only seven of the batch of twenty N.T.5s still survived in service; by October 1918, they had all gone.

Specification

Type:	N.T.5 Flying Boat
Date:	1916-1918
Seats:	Two
Power:	100 h.p. Gnôme Monosoupape rotary
	130 hp Clerget
Dimensions:	
Length:	28 ft. 8 in.
Height:	9 ft. 9 in.
Span, upper:	44 ft. 0 in.
Span, lower:	33 ft. 7 in.
Chord, upper:	5 ft. 6 in.
Chord, lower:	4 ft. 3 in.
Gap:	5 ft. 3 in.
Stagger:	4¼ in.
Wing area:	358 sq. ft.
Wing loading:	5.42 lbs. per sq. ft.
Weight, empty:	1,231 lbs.
loaded:	1,950 lbs.
Performance:	
Maximum speed:	60 m.p.h.
Endurance:	4 hours
Tank capacities:	
Petrol:	36 gallons
Oil:	10 gallons
Propeller:	Four-bladed, 2,600 mm diameter
Armament:	One Lewis gun; light bombs

N.T.5 N1052 (right) at Lee-on-Solent seaplane station in April 1918

Production and Serial Numbers

N1040/N1059	20	Contract C.P.120948/16
3201, 3206,	4	Hulls only
9607, 9608		

Ten hulls built as spares

Service History

N1040   Completed January 1917; deld to Calshot 10.2.17; deleted by 5.10.17

N1041   Completed 3.2.17; deld to Killingholme 27.3.17; to training aircraft ; deleted by 5.10.17

N1042   Completed 10.3.17; delivered to Killingholme 27.3.17; to training aircraft; deleted by 6.4.18

N1043   Completed 31.3.17; deld to Calshot 4.4.17; deleted 11.7.17

N1044   Completed 31.3.17; deld to Killingholme 3.4.17 for erection; Calshot School 11.7.17; crashed 11.10.17 and pilot killed; surveyed 8.11.17 and deleted 17.11.17

N1045   Deld to Killingholme 3.4.17 for erection; to training aircraft by 23.12.17; 209 TDS Lee-on-Solent by 6.6.18; deleted by 25.7.18

N1046   Deld to Killingholme 10.4.17 for erection; damaged on test and retd seriously damaged to Mkrs 17.5.17; Calshot School 26.7.17; surveyed 28.9.17 and deleted 6.10.17

N1047   Fitted 100 hp Gnôme; completed 21.4.17; deld to Calshot School 8.6.17; Lee-on-Solent by 12.10.17; surveyed 30.10.17; deleted 6.11.17

N1048   Completed April 1917; deld to Calshot School 28.6.17; wrecked 11.9.17; Lee-on-Solent by 12.10.17; surveyed 30.10.17 and deleted 6.11.17

N1049   Completed April 1917; deld to Calshot School 16.6.17; wrecked 28.6.17; surveyed 28.9.18 and deleted 6.10.17

N1050   Completed 31.3.17; deld to Calshot School 4.17; wrecked on landing 12.4.17; deleted 25.4.17

N1051   Fitted 100 hp Gnôme; completed 31.3.17; force-landed, Bembridge, 5.4.17 en route to Calshot; arr Calshot 6.4.17 coded H; Lee by 30.11.17; deleted 27.3.18

N1052   C/n 261; completed 7.4.17; deld to Calshot School 19.4.17; Lee-on-Solent by 3.18; became 209 TDS 1.4.18l crashed 5.18 and deleted by 11.7.18

N1053   Completed 7.4.17; deld to Calshot School 19.4.17; deleted by 1.3.18

N1054   Completed 14.4.17; deld to Calshot School 5.4.17; surveyed 14.9.17 and deleted by 1.3.18

N1055   Completed 21.4.17; deld to Calshot School 8.6.17; found DBR 14.9.17; surveyed 3.11.17 and deleted 8.11.17

N.T.5 N1059 at Calshot

N1056   Completed 28.4.17; deld to Calshot School 12.6.17; surveyed 28.9.17 and deleted 6.10.17

N1057   Completed 28.4.17; deld to Calshot School 12.6.17; crashed and DBR 11.7.17; deleted 15.7.17

N1058   Completed 26.5.17; deld to Calshot School 24.5.17; possibly aircraft in which pilot drowned 3.10.17; surveyed 7.10.17 and deleted 10.10.17 as wrecked

N1059   Fitted 100 hp Gnôme; deld to Calshot School 24.5.17; surveyed 3.11.17 and deleted 8.11.17

Crew accommodation and engine lay-out on an N.T.5

N.T.2B N2575 alighting off Lee-on-Solent

CHAPTER 10

The N.T.2B Flying Boats

The Admiralty's decision to standardise on twin-engined flying boats of the Porte/Felixstowe type for patrol duties meant that Norman Thompson had to find an attractive design in a category still required by the R.N.A.S., or possibly by the R.F.C., contracts for which would provide work in the recently enlarged factories at Middleton and Littlehampton.

Percy Beadle's redesigned hull for the N.T.2A had proved to be strong and to have good take-off characteristics; it was therefore decided that this would provide the basis for a two-seater flying boat basic trainer for R.N.A.S. pilots, who would then graduate to the Porte boats. The F.B.A.s currently being used had good handling qualities in the air but their hulls were rather fragile and could not long stand up to the rough usage of "circuits and bumps".

Drawings of the new trainer, to be known as the N.T.2B, were quickly prepared and submitted to the Admiralty on 27 October 1916 and an experimental machine, fitted with a 140 h.p. Hispano-Suiza engine, was built as a private venture and was completed and ready for trials by 27 January 1917. This machine was purchased by the Admiralty for £1,000 plus the cost of the hull and was given the serial number N26. Unfortunately, at about this time, Thompsons had some labour unrest and were faced with a demand from their workers

for one penny per hour more pay because Wells Aviation Company had established a factory at Bosham and were offering higher wages to induce suitable tradesmen to join them. N26 was eventually delivered to Calshot on 5 April 1917 for type trials.

Meanwhile, an initial order for ten machines, plus spares, was received on 10 November 1916 and these were allocated serial numbers N1180 - N1189. Detail drawings were completed by 22 December and a mock-up of the enclosed cockpit was then being made. The totally-enclosed cabin provided comfortable side-by-side seating for the instructor and pupil. Dual control-wheels and rudder pedals were fitted. The two-bay wings were of unequal span, with upper extensions which were braced from kingposts fitted above the outer interplane struts. The kingposts were faired by fabric-covered fins of semi-circular shape. Ailerons were fitted to the top wing and projected behind the trailing-edge; there was also a cut-out for the propeller. Stabilising floats were attached to the lower wing, immediately under the outboard interplane struts. Beaching wheels could be attached to the base of the hull just aft of the wing leading-edge and a skid was fitted under the stern-post.

The first hull was completed by the end of January 1917 but final delivery was delayed by discussions over the desirability of changing the

N.T.2A built as a private venture prototype for the N.T.2B and later bought by the Admiralty as N26

type of engine to be used. The first batch was to have been fitted with the 120 h.p. Beardmore engines and N1180 - N1183 were apparently delivered in June 1917 with this installation and with a four-bladed propeller. However, by now it had been decided by the Admiralty that a more powerful engine was required and the remainder of the original batch, N1184 - N1189, were fitted between July and October 1917 with 150 h.p. Hispano-Suizas driving a two-bladed propeller.

A second contract was awarded to Norman Thompson later in 1917; this was for 25 machines which were serialled N2555 - N2579. Deliveries commenced in December 1917 and the first two or three were fitted with the 150 h.p. Hispano. Most of the remainder were to have had 200 h.p. Hispanos but were delivered direct to store after completion without engines being fitted. As Norman Thompson's capacity was, in theory, fully committed, contracts were also awarded to Saunders (for 24 machines numbered N2500 - N2523) and to Supermarine (75 machines).

A few of the second batch built by Norman Thompsons were test flown with the larger Hispano and the more powerful torque, as compared with the smaller Hispano and Beardmore, caused problems with longitudinal control, This was solved by mounting the engine slightly to the starboard of the centre line. However, Hispano engines were in considerable demand for fighter aircraft and a substitute was therefore required. The 200 h.p. Sunbeam Arab was selected and output at Norman Thompson, Saunders and Supermarine was stopped in June 1918 for about six weeks whilst engine bearers were modified to take Arabs in place of Hispanos. Unfortunately, however, the Arab did not

take kindly to its installation as a pusher unit and there were endless problems with engine failures. Saunders eventually completely dismantled an Arab and found that there was no proper thrust bearing for use as a pusher. By the end of July, Saunders' works were cluttered with N.T.2Bs which were complete except for their engines and could not be flown away until the Sunbeam Arabs could be persuaded to run properly.

The four-bladed propeller fitted to the Arab was also found to be unsuitable and caused overheating to the back plate of the propeller hub. It was suggested that a light two-blader, as fitted to 200 h.p. Hispano-Suizas on Tellier flying boats, might be worth trying. The torque problems were also evident with the Arab installation and eventually a form of slewed engine mounting was produced which cured the trouble.

Because of delays, the Admiralty attempted to cancel the Supermarine contract for 75 machines on 14 October but were too late as the company had already produced all the metal fittings and had purchased the timber. It was therefore agreed that the 75 machines would be fitted with Sunbeam Arabs as and when they became available. Partly to balance the books, a contract for 29 Sage School seaplanes was cancelled instead.

Although a total of 295 N.T.2Bs was ordered as the R.N.A.S./R.A.F. standard flying boat trainer, the continual mechanical problems so delayed deliveries that very few machines had actually entered service by the time the War ended and several of the contracts were drastically cut back. It would appear that the total actually built was 156; of these, a large number went into store at South Shotwick, Norwich and Sherburn. Others were

N.T.2B N1181 with a 120 hp Beardmore engine

retained at Bognor pending resale for export. The hold-up in deliveries of the N.T.2B had a serious effect on the elementary training of flying boat crews who were desperately needed to fly as second pilots in the increasing numbers of F-boats which were being delivered to R.A.F. units in 1918. Those that actually saw service were mainly based at Calshot and Lee-on-Solent.

The Handley Page subsidiary, the Aircraft Disposal Company, handled the sale of most of the surplus N.T.2Bs and fitted many of them with 200 h.p. Wolseley Viper engines. On 6 December 1920 they ordered all but twenty of them to be scrapped. Various opportunities were taken to advertise the N.T.2B as a light flying boat for the private owner, survey companies or local airlines. These included N2282 which was shown at the Atlantic City Exposition in 1919, N2294 which was exhibited at Harrods also in 1919 and N2268 which was included in the Imperial War Museum display of aircraft at the Crystal Palace in June 1920, where it was shown floating in one of the ponds in the centre of the Great Hall.

Of the N.T.2Bs which were exported, three went to Canada. G-CACH (ex N2290 and G-EAQO) was registered to Rocky Mountain Aviation Transport Company, Banff, Alberta, in June 1921 and was flown from Lake Minnewanka. The smooth fresh water of the lake was of no help to the take-off characteristics and, in an effort to improve them, wooden sponsons were fitted to the forepart of the hull. In June 1924, G-CACG was transferred to Dominion Aerial Exploration Company, Toronto, and flown from Roberval, Quebec and Oslo in the Lake St.John region. The registration was cancelled in August 1924 and presumably the machine was scrapped. G-CAEL (original serial not known) was also registered to Dominion Aerial Exploration in June 1924 and was transferred to J.V.Elliott Air

Service, Hamilton, Ontario, in June 1926. It was scrapped at Hamilton in September 1929. G-CAEM (ex N2573) was also registered to Dominion in June 1924 and may only have been used to provide spares for 'CG and 'EL.

Two machines were sold to Peru in 1919, probably for aerial survey and transport work; these were originally serialled N2284 and N2293. On their arrival in Peru, presumably because of the hot weather, the cabin tops were removed, leaving only the windscreens.

The Estonian Government bought two N.T.2Bs (ex N2286 and N2287) in May 1919 and these were numbered 7 and 8 on arrival.

Three went to Norway (ex N2288, N2275 and N2266) and were re-serialled N.12, N.13 and N.14. One went to Russia in 1922 and was used for communications. For part of the time it was operated on skis.

N2283 went to Japan, N2282, N2285, N2292, N2405 and N2410 were also exported to unknown destinations.

A number of surplus hulls were converted into motor launches and cabin cruisers by the Rampart Boat Company and fitted with 8-10 h.p. single-cylinder Siemens engines which have them a speed of 16 m.p.h.

Given the right engine and produced at the right time, the comfortable little N.T.2B might have made a good name for itself as an elementary flying boat trainer.

Specification

Trials report: Arab NM211 15.8.18

Type:	N.T.2B Flying Boat
Date:	1917 - 1920
Seats:	Two

N.T.2B N1185 with a 150 hp Hispano-Suiza engine

Power:
140 h.p. Hispano-Suiza (N26)
120 h.p. Beardmore Austro-Daimler (N1180/1183)
160 h.p. Beardmore Austro-Daimler
200 h.p. Sunbeam Arab
150 h.p. Hispano-Suiza
200 h.p. Hispano-Suiza
200 h.p. Wolseley Viper

Dimensions:

Length	27 ft. 4½ in.
Height:	10 ft. 8 in.
Span, upper:	48 ft. 4½ in.
Span, lower:	27 ft. 6½ in.
Chord:	5 ft. 6 in.
Gap:	5 ft. 6 in.
Incidence:	5 degrees
Dihedral:	1 degree
Wing area:	453 sq. ft.

Weights:

	Arab	Viper (civil)
Empty:	2,521 lbs.	2,050 lbs.
Loaded:	3,169 lbs	2,910 lbs.

Performance:

	Arab	Viper
Max. speed at 2,000 ft:	85 mph.	86.5 mph.
at 5,400 ft;	83.5 mph	84.5 mph
at 10,000 ft:	80.5 mph	82.5 mph

Climb to 2,000 ft	4 min. 10 sec.
5,000 ft	11 min. 55 sec.
6,500 ft	16 min. 50 sec.
8,000 ft	23 min. 0 sec.
10,000 ft	33 min. 40 sec.

Ceiling: 11,400 ft.   14, 000 ft.

Tank capacity:

Petrol	60 gallons
Oil	8 gallons

Armament: Two 100-lb bombs

Costs:

N.26	£1,000 minus hull;
N1180/9	£1,350 each.
N2500/23	£1,200 (trolley £38.50) each;
N2555/798	Ten @ £1,450, 25 @ £1,400 each.
N2760/84	£1,400 each.
Six spare hulls	£693 each

Production and Serial Numbers

Probably 156 actually completed (see below).

N26	1	Contract A.S.4682 (BR255)
N1180/1189	10	Contract A.S.133705/16
N2260/2359	100	Contract A.S.24906/18 (BR595) 35 built
N2400/2429	30	Contract A.S.17694/18 (BR447) 38a/400/C396
N2500/2523	24	Contract A.S.22028/1/17 (BR154) 15 built by S.E. Saunders
N2555/2579	25	Contract A.S.25834/18 (BR177)
N2760/2789	30	Contract A.S.34279/18 (BR248) 25 built by Supermarine
N3300/3374	75	Contract A.S.26371/18 (Br627) 38a/612/C641 15 built by Supermarine

Service History

N26   Completed January 1917; Calshot 5.4.17; Grain January 1918; Calshot 11.1.18; written off at Calshot 1.3.18

N1180   Hull completed January 1917; delivered to Calshot School 8.6.17; surveyed 18.12.17 and deleted 28.12.17

N1181   Delivered to Calshot School 18.6.17; 209 TDS Lee-on-Solent by 6.18; fitted with 150 hp HS

N1182   Delivered to Calshot School 30.6.17; for deletion by 2.2.18

N1183   Delivered to Calshot School 22.7.17; Cherbourg 24.7.17; wrecked in hangar destroyed in gale, 28.8.17; deleted 14.9.17

N1184   Delivered to Calshot School 25.7.17; deleted 29.10.17 as wrecked

N1185   Delivered to Calshot School 20.7.17; deleted 21.11.17 as wrecked

N1186   Delivered to Calshot School by 8.17; for deletion by 30.3.18

N1187   Delivered to Calshot School by 6.17; Lee-on-Solent by 12.10.17; Calshot School by 2.11.17; for deletion by 22.2.18

N1188   Delivered to Calshot School by 7.17; for deletion by 22.3.18

N1189   Fitted 150 hp HS; Lee-on-Solent by October 1917; became 209 TDS 1.4.18; deleted 8.8.18

N2260   Delivered 2.11.18 to 209 TDS Lee-on-Solent 31.12.18 to 1.19

N2261   Delivered 2.11.18 to 209 TDS Lee-on-Solent 31.12.18 to 1.19

N2262   Delivered 9.11.18 to 209 TDS Lee-on-Solent 31.12.18 to 1.19

N2263   Delivered 9.11.18 to 209 TDS Lee-on-Solent 31.12.18 to 1.19

N2264   Delivered 16.11.18 to 209 TDS Lee-on-Solent 31.12.18 to 1.19

N2265   Delivered 16.11.18 to 209 TDS Lee-on-Solent 31.12.18 to 1.19

N2266   Delivered 23.11.18 to store at South Shotwick; C of A 295 issued 30.1.20 and exported to Norway as N-14

N2267   Delivered 23.11.18 to 209 TDS Lee-on-Solent 31.12.18 to 1.19

N2268   Delivered 23.11.18 to 209 TDS Lee-on-Solent 31.12.18 to 10.19; at Crystal Palace 1920

N2269   Delivered 23.11.18 to 209 TDS Lee-on-Solent

N2270   Delivered 7.12.18 to 209 TDS Lee-on-Solent

N2271   Delivered 7.12.18 to 209 TDS Lee-on-Solent

N2272   Delivered 7.12.18 to 209 TDS Lee-on-Solent

N2273   Delivered 7.12.18 to 209 TDS Lee-on-Solent

N2274   Retained at Bognor 17.10.18; at Bognor 31.12.18 for disposal

N2275   At Bognor 31.12.18 for disposal to S.W. Area; C of A 289 issued 11.1.20; exported to Norway as N.12 and regd to A Meisterlin, Oslo, 22.6.20; sold to C Groos, Son in 1924 and cancelled 17.10.25; Possibly regd N-27 20.10.25 to C Groos and cancelled 25.2.29 but see N2288 below

N2276   At Bognor 31.12.18 for 209 TDS

N2277   At Bognor 31.12.18 for 209 TDS

N2278   At Bognor 31.12.18 for 209 TDS

N2279   At Bognor 31.12.18 for S.W. Area

N2280   At Bognor 31.12.18 for S.W. Area

N2281   Stored at South Shotwick by 1.19; possibly exported

N2282   Stored at South Shotwick by 1.19; C of A 280 issued 20.12.19 and exported early 1920

N2283   Stored at makers; C of A 260 issued 7.11.19 and exported to Japan

N2284   Stored at makers; C of A 264 issued 18.11.39 and sold to Peru; at Atlantic City Exposition in 1919

N2285   Stored at makers; C of A 273 issued 2.12.19 and exported early 1920

N2286   Stored at makers; to Estonian Government in May 1919

N2287   Stored at makers; to Estonian Government in May 1919

N2288   Stored at makers; issued exported to Norway as N-13 and regd 22.6.20 to A Meisterlin; possibly rebuilt in 1925 as (part of?) N-27 as identity quoted as "2288" (but also see N2275)

N2289   No record

N2290   To civil register as G-EAQO; to Canada and regd under C of R 80 on 9.6.21 to Rocky Mountain Aviation, Banff, Alta. as G-CACG. Re-regd No.249 21.5.24 to Dominion Aerial Exploration, Toronto. Cancelled 31.8.26

N2291   Probably sold abroad

N2292   Probably sold abroad

N2293   C of A 271 issued 28.11.39 and sold to Peru

N2294   Fitted with Beardmore, later 200 hp Arab; exhibited at Harrods in 1919

N2296 to N2359 All cancelled January 1919

N2400   Delivered to Calshot by 5.18; Grain A.C.D. 4.8.18 for type and prop tests

N2401   Delivered 29.8.18 to 209 TDS Lee-on-Solent to 1.19

N2402   Delivered 29.8.18 to 209 TDS Lee-on-Solent to 1.19

N2403   Delivered 8.18 into store at MAD Sherburn-in-Elmet to 1.19

N2404   Delivered 31.8.18 into store at Brockworth to 1.19

N2405   Delivered 26.9.18 into store at South Shotwick to 1.19; C of A 288 issued 9.1.20

N2406   Delivered 26.9.18 into store at South Shotwick to 1.19

N2407   Delivered 76.9.18 into store at South Shotwick to 1.19

N2408   Delivered 26.9.18 into store at South Shotwick to 1.19

N2409   Delivered 26.9.18 into store at South Shotwick to 1.19

N2410   Delivered 26.9.18 into store at South Shotwick to 1.19; C of A 286 issued 1.1.20 and then exported

N2411   Delivered 26.9.18 into store at South Shotwick to 1.19

N2412   Delivered by 31.10.18 into store at MAD Sherburn-in-Elmet, 17.10.18 to 1.19

N2413   Delivered by 31.10.18 into store at MAD Sherburn-in-Elmet to 1.19

N2414   Delivered 28.9.18; into store at 3 AAP Norwich, 17.10.18 to 1.19

N2415   Delivered 28.9.18; into store at 3 AAP Norwich, 17.10.18 to 1.19

N2416   Delivered 28.9.18; into store at 3 AAP Norwich, 17.10.18 to 1.19

N2417   Delivered by 31.10.18 into store at MAD Sherburn-in-Elmet, 17.10.18 to 1.19

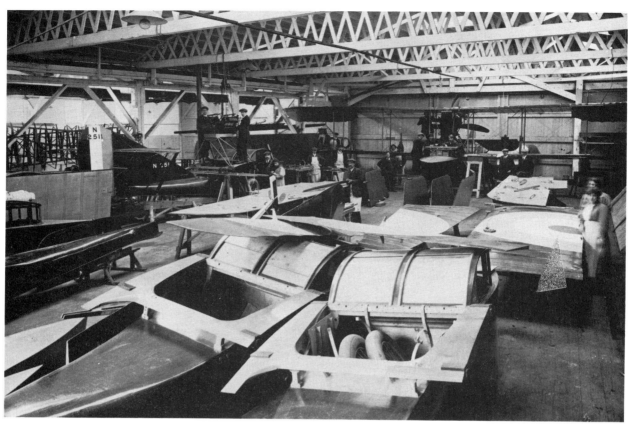

N.T.2Bs under construction at S. E. Saunders, East Cowes

N2418   Delivered by 31.10.18 into store at MAD Sherburn-in-Elmet, 17.10.18 to 1.19

N2419   Delivered by 31.10.18 into store at MAD Sherburn-in-Elmet, 17.10.18 to 1.19

N2420   Delivered by 31.10.18 into store at MAD Sherburn-in-Elmet, 17.10.18 to 1.19

N2421   Delivered 12.10.18 to 209 TDS Lee-on-Solent 17.10.18 to 1.19

N2421   Delivered 12.10.18 to 209 TDS Lee-on-Solent 17.10.18 to 1.19

N2422   Delivered 12.10.18 to 209 TDS Lee-on-Solent 17.10.18 to 1.19

N2423   Delivered 11.18 into store at MAD Sherburn-in-Elmet to 1.19

N2424   Delivered 11.18 into store at MAD Sherburn-in-Elmet to 1.19

N2425   Delivered 10.18 to 209 TDS Lee-on-Solent 17.10.18 to 1.19

N2426   Delivered 10.18 to 209 TDS Lee-on-Solent 17.10.18 to 1.19

N2427   Delivered 10.18 to 209 TDS Lee-on-Solent 17.10.18 to 1.19

N2428   Delivered 10.18 to 209 TDS Lee-on-Solent 17.10.18 to 1.19

N2429   Delivered 10.18 to 209 TDS Lee-on-Solent 17.10.18 to 1.19

N2500   Delivered for trials at Lee-on-Solent 20.4.18; Calshot School by 25.5.18; 209 TDS Lee-on-Solent 17.10.18 to 1.19

N2501   Fitted with 200 hp HS; Newport store 18.5.18; Calshot School by 27.6.18; ARS Calshot 25.7.18 to 1.19

N2502   Delivered 1.6.18 to Calshot for trials; Calshot School by 25.5.18; to store 1.19

N2503   Delivered 15.6.18 for storage at 1 SD Newport; allotted Calshot School by 25.5.18; Saunders 23.11.18; 209 TDS by 1.19

N2504   Delivered 22.6.18 for storage at 1 SD Newport; 209 TDS Lee-on-Solent by 11.18 to 1.19

N2505   Delivered 29.10.18 to 209 TDS Lee-on-Solent to 1.19

N2506   Delivered 17.10.18 to 209 TDS Lee-on-Solent to 1.19

N2507   Delivered to 1 (S) MAD Hamble for storage 17.10.18; to S.W. Area for disposal 31.12.18

N2508   Delivered 19.10.18 to 209 TDS Lee-on-Solent to 1.19

N2509   Delivered 26.10.18 to 1 (S) MAD Hamble; 209 TDS Lee-on-Solent 11.18 to 1.19

N2510 to N2514 Built but no record of delivery

N2515 to N2523 Cancelled 6.19

N2555   Delivered to Calshot School by 19.12.17; for deletion by 5.4.18

N2556   Delivered to Calshot School by 29.12.17; ARS Calshot for ISD storage by 25.7.18 to 1.19

N2557   Delivered 15.1.18 to Calshot School; Eastleigh store by 25.7.18; AAP South Shotwick 26.9.18 to 1.19

N2558   Delivered to Calshot School by 2.2.18; 209 TDS Lee-on-Solent by 10.18 to 1.19

N2559   Delivered 27.1.18 to Dover; Grain Type Test Flt 28.1.18 for type and prop tests and fabric evaluation; deleted 12.12.18

N2560   Delivered to Grain ECD by 5.2.18; for disposal 8.20

N2561   Delivered to Calshot by 8.3.18; to training by 7.18; to storage at South Shotwick by 26.9.18 to 1.19

N2562   Delivered to Calshot School 24.2.18; 209 TDS by 27.5.18; deleted 7.11.18

N2563   Delivered to Calshot School by 8.3.18; in storage at Eastleigh by 25.7.18; AAP South Shotwick by 26.9.18 to 1.19

N2564   Delivered to Calshot School by 8.3.18; in storage Eastleigh by 25.7.18; AAP South Shotwick 26.9.18 to 1.19

N2565   Delivered to Calshot School by 3.18; in storage Eastleigh by 25.7.18; AAP South Shotwick 26.9.18 to 1.19

N2566   Delivered to Calshot School by 3.18; in storage Eastleigh by 25.7.18; AAP South Shotwick 26.9.18 to 1.19

N2567   Delivered to Calshot School by 3.18; in storage Eastleigh by 25.7.18; AAP South Shotwick 26.9.18 to 1.19

N2568   Delivered to Calshot School by 3.18; in storage at Calshot by 10.18 to 1.19

N2569   First aircraft with slewed engine installation; delivered 30.3.18 to Calshot School; ISD storage at Calshot 25.7.18 to 1.19

N2570   Delivered to Calshot School by 4.18; in storage Eastleigh by 25.7.18; AAP South Shotwick 4.9.18 to 1.19

N2571   Delivered to Calshot School by 4.18; in storage Eastleigh by 25.7.18; AAP South Shotwick 4.9.18 to 1.19

N2572   Delivered to Calshot School by 4.18; in storage Eastleigh by 25.7.18; AAP South Shotwick 4.9.18 to 1.19

N2573   Delivered to Calshot School by 5.18; in storage Eastleigh by 25.7.18; AAP South Shotwick 4.9.18 to 1.19; to Canada as G-CAEM for Dominion Aerial Exploration. Not regd and used for spares. Sold 1928 to J V Elliott Air Service; scrapped 1929

N2574   Delivered 25.5.18 to Calshot School; 209 TDS Lee-on-Solent by 27.6.18 to 1.19

N2575   Delivered 25.5.18 to Calshot School; 209 TDS Lee-on-Solent by 27.6.18 to 1.19

N2576   Delivered 25.5.18 to Calshot School; ISD storage at Calshot 25.7.18 to 1.19

N2577   Delivered 25.5.18 to Calshot School; ISD storage at Calshot 25.7.18 to 1.19

N2578   Fitted with Arab; delivered 18.5.18 to Calshot for trials then to School; to storage 27.6.18; storage at AAP South Shotwick 26.9.18 to 1.19

N2579   Fitted with Arab; delivered 18.5.18 to Calshot for trials then to School; to storage 27.6.18; storage at AAP South Shotwick 26.9.18 to 1.19

N2760   Delivered 4.4.18 to Lee-on-Solent; Calshot School by 27.4.18; ARS Calshot for ISD store 10.18 to 1.19

N2761 to N2778   Delivered to store 5.8.18; at Munitions Store 17.10.18 to 1.19

N2779 to N2784   Delivered but remained in storage 5.8.18

N2785 to N2789   Cancelled

N3300 to N3314   None delivered to 2.12.18; possibly built in 1919

N3315 to N3374   Cancelled December 1918

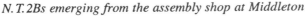

N.T.2Bs emerging from the assembly shop at Middleton

N.T.2B G-CACG (ex-N2268) on Lake Minnewanka, Alberta
N.T.2B N2268 on show at Crystal Palace in 1920

N2266 from the second production batch

N.T.2B N2569 from the fifth batch

Cabin and engine installation on N.T.2B

N.T.2B exported to Russia

G-CAEL at Roberval, Quebec

N2294 ready for delivery at Middleton

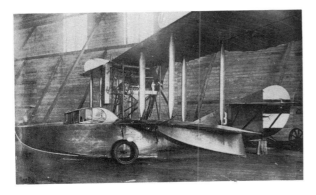

N.T.2B exported to Estonia

Completed N.T.2B hull at East Cowes

The Tandem Norman Thompson at Middleton

CHAPTER 11

The TNT Flying Boat Fighter

Admiralty Air Department Category N.1b issued in 1917 gave a specification for a single-engined high performance flying boat or seaplane fighting scout. Several companies produced prototypes in this category, for example Supermarine, Blackburn and Westland; Norman Thompson, by now with considerable experience of flying boat hull construction, decided to submit a design which would also conform to the specification of the N.2a category.

The design evidently found favour with the Air Department, possibly because although compact in size, it was a two-seater and thus offered more flexibility in operation. An order for a single prototype was placed on 24 April 1917 and Norman Thompson's tender price of £1,485 was accepted.

The single-stepped hull was similar in construction to that of the N.T.2B but was slightly shorter. The two open cockpits were in tandem forward of the lower wing and each was fitted with a transparent windscreen.

The two-bay unstaggered wings were of equal span and were arranged to fold forwards, being hinged at the front spar. The ailerons, fitted to both upper and lower wings, were initially connected by

thin struts but these were subsequently replaced by cables. The trailing-edge of the centre-section was cut away to allow the propeller to revolve. The large fin and rudder was unlike anything previously fitted to Norman Thompson flying boats and had a high-mounted tailplane braced with two struts on each side.

The high-mounted 200 h.p. Hispano engine drove a large four-bladed pusher propeller; for many years this propeller was in the possession of the Bromley, Kent, furnishing store, Dunns of Bromley. A car-type radiator was fitted in front of the engine and the starting crank handle protruded through it.

Large stabilising floats were fitted just inboard of the lower wing-tips. There was no provision for fitting beaching-wheels to an axle pushed through the hull as in the N.T.2B; instead, a normal separate beaching trolley was used.

Construction started immediately on receipt of the contract and no doubt the TNT (Tandem Norman Thompson) utilised a number of fittings already being produced for the N.T.2B. By July, the components had entered the erecting shop and the TNT was completed in September. Early in

N37 at Middleton. Note the strut linking ailerons

October, it was launched for its preliminary trials amidst the interest and great excitement of the whole works.

The first flight, by Clifford Prodger, was a great success and the little flying boat was found to have splendid climbing power and high speed - 96 knots uncorrected and climb to 10,000 feet in 18½ minutes. In November, it went back into the factory for alterations which were intended to improve the top speed.

The Air Department reported that with full N.2a load it was expected to do slightly better than the A.D. Flying Boat but that the TNT was much smaller and it was not expected that the hull would stand as much rough usage under service conditions. However, the firm's trials in rough water seem to have disproved this suggestion and the hull was found to be very strong. An officer from the Air Department visited Middleton and carefully examined the TNT with regard to the strength of the tail. The designer stated that the only weakness had been in the aerial structure which had been stiffened with another cross-strut.

The TNT was given the serial number N37 and was then accepted by the Admiralty in December 1917. It went to the Isle of Grain Test Flight and arrived there on 19 December for its official trials.

In January 1918, the hull was damaged but trials continued after the damage was repaired.

The official Trial Report NM173 was dated 18 May 1918 and stated:

Manoeuvrability:	Good
Longitudinal Stability:	Unstable when varying throttle
Lateral Stability:	Stable
Directional Stability:	Stable but swings when using throttle
Control - Longitudinal:	Good but tail heavy with engine throttled
Control - Lateral:	Good
Control - Directional:	Good
Control - Taxying:	Not good in wind

Machine takes a long time to get off the water owing to too small a hull.

The performance figures were found to be inferior in all respects to those obtained from the original makers' trials and, in common with the other machines built to the N.1b specification, the TNT was not adopted for quantity production and saw no active service.

By October 1918, it was no longer on charge with the R.A.F.

Specification

Type:	TNT (Tandem Norman Thompson) N.1b Flying Boat
Date:	1918
Seats:	Two
Power:	150 Hispano-Suiza 8A
	200 h.p. Hispano 8B

Dimensions

Length:	26 ft.5 in. (folded 32 ft.8 in.)
Height:	9 ft.7 in.

Span: 34 ft.3 in. (folded 13 ft.2 in.)

Performance

Max speed at 2,000 ft: 93 m.p.h.
Max speed at 6,500 ft: 92 m.p.h.
Max speed at 10,000 feet: 86.5 m.p.h.
Climb to 2,000 ft: 3 min.30 sec.
Climb to 5,000 ft: 10 min.6 sec.
Climb to 6,500 ft: 14 min.20 sec.
Climb to 10,000 ft: 27 min.35 sec.
Ceiling: 12,600 ft
Armament: Probably one Lewis gun
Cost: £1,485

Production:

One aircraft, N37; Contract A.S.10732/17 (BR64)

Service history

N37   Completed October 1917; to Type Test
       Dept Grain 20.12.17; re-engined 200 HS
       engine; damaged on landing 1.18; deleted
       by 27.6.18

The Tandem Norman Thompson

Short S.38 No.8437 built by Norman Thompson

CHAPTER 12

Unbuilt Projects and Production for other Companies

The Norman Thompson Company produced a number of designs which, for one reason or another, were never built or, if commenced, were not completed.

An Admiralty Air Department contract (C.P.67552/15) was awarded in 1915 for the supply of 20 machines of an unknown type; these were allocated the serial numbers 1280 - 1299. It is possible that the contract was for N.T.2s or N.T.2As and that it was cancelled when the R.N.A.S. requirement was altered in favour of twin-engined flying boats for anti-submarine patrol duties. Alternatively, this may have been for a small single-seater flying boat with wireless and a 150 h.p. Sunbeam engine and able to take off from carrier decks on a trolley. A further order for twelve flying bpoats serialled 1497 - 1508 was also awarded in 1915 but was soon cancelled.

N.T.6 was a design for twin-engined Air Cruisers undertaken at the request of the Admiralty in 1916 for which a trial order (AS 24382) was given on 5 January 1917 for two experimental machines serialled N18 and N19. Drawings and stressing were completed and work had just begun in the shops when a change of policy forced the Admiralty to cancel the order on 10 December 1917. It is assumed that this was to have been a

long-range flying boat. Two 320 h.p. Sunbeam engines would have been fitted.

N.T.7 was a design, ordered by the Naval Section of the Air Ministry early in 1918, for a school flying boat for training naval pilots and allotted order number AS 7758/BR367. The serial numbers were to have been N108 - N109 but the order was cancelled on 21 April 1918 before the drawings were completed in detail and the N.T.2B was finally adopted as the standard flying boat trainer. The engine was to have been a 150 h.p. or 200 h.p. Hispano-Suiza or a 200 h.p. Sunbeam Arab.

Mention has already been made of a suggestion by the firm to fit three 200 h.p. engines to the N.2c flying boat. It would appear that they were also asked to look at the design of a large flying boat in the N.3a category with 200 h.p. engines and calculations were carried out in 1918.

The rapid expansion of the R.N.A.S. in 1915 led to the Admiralty placing increased orders for basic trainers for use at Eastchurch and Chingford Flying Schools and, because of their satisfaction with the earlier Short Biplanes, they wished to standardise on the Short S.38. However, by then Shorts were fully committed with the production of floatplanes and the orders were placed with other

Short No.8434 at Farnborough

contractors. Supermarine were given a contract for twelve and White and Thompson received three contracts totalling 24 machines. Deliveries were completed by June 1916; the heavy wear and tear of daily training flights meant that, by January 1917, they had all been written off.

Williams of Littlehampton built at least eight Felixstowe F.2a hulls in 1917/18 against contract AS 13309, probably as sub-contractors to May, Harden and May at Hythe.

It has been reported that Norman Thompson were considered as potential constructors of the Vickers F.B.27 Vimy but, by then, the Company's finances were in such a state that they were not ultimately awarded a contract.

Short No.3144

Porte and Hallett in the Curtiss H.1

CHAPTER 13

John Cyril Porte - Hero or Rogue? - The 1917 Conspiracy Trial

Sir Walter Raleigh in Volume 1 of "The War in the Air" wrote: "The shortest possible list of those who served their country in its hour of need would have to include his name". He was, of course, referring to John Cyril Porte. And yet, only three years before, Commander Porte had stood in the dock at the Central Criminal Court facing fifteen counts of corruptly receiving illegal commission whilst holding office as a servant of the Crown. How did this happen?

John Porte was born on 26 February 1884 at Bandon, Co.Cork, and in 1898 he entered the Royal Navy as a cadet in HMS *Britannia*, the Royal Naval College at Dartmouth. After his initial training, he volunteered for the submarine service and was posted to the depot ships HMS *Thames* and HMS *Forth* for instruction. On 1 January 1908 he was appointed to command the submarine *B3* and on 31 March 1910 he went to the modern submarine *C38* as captain and seemed well set for a highly successful career in the Navy. However, this was not to be as an unexpected physical weakness, perhaps triggered by long hours in the cold and wet of an exposed submarine bridge, was eventually diagnosed as pulmonary tuberculosis and he was therefore invalided out of the Navy early in 1911. Luckily, by then Porte had found another absorbing interest and built a glider of unusual layout, which was tested on a wooden track down the north side of Portsdown Hill. The complications of its two-man control system soon led to a crash in which it was

written-off. However, Porte, undeterred, carried on experimenting and built his own version of the Santos-Dumont Demoiselle in 1910 and also a biplane with a tubular steel frame and a 40 h.p Green engine. On leaving the Navy, he was therefore well prepared to start a new career in aviation, no doubt feeling that a life spent largely in the fresh air would be beneficial to his health. At that time the facilities for flying instruction were better in France and so he went to Reims where he gained his Aero Club de France Certificate No.548 on a Deperdussin Monoplane. His instructors had such a regard for his skill as a "natural pilot" that he was recommended to the newly-formed British Deperdussin Company and was soon appointed as their Technical Director and test pilot. The monoplanes built by the Company incorporated many design improvements suggested by Porte and were successfully flown by him at races and flying displays throughout Britain, at which he won many prizes.

His first association with waterplanes came in 1913 when Deperdussin designed and built a floatplane called the *Seagull*. This was a monoplane fitted with a 100 h.p. Anzani engine and an order for two of them was received from the Admiralty.

Although it was reported as being "a delight to handle and very soothing", other sources say that it was eventually refused by the Navy following unsuccessful trials caused by the engine being insufficiently powerful for take-off except when conditions were perfect. It seems that the company was already in a shaky financial condition and the cancellation of the *Seagull* order was the final blow which drove them out of business in August 1913. Porte thereby lost his job and the money which he had invested in the Company. The chief debenture holder in the firm was Admiral Freemantle and he asked a barrister, William Augustus Casson, to take possession as Receiver and wind up the Company. Casson was an old friend of the Porte family, possibly even one of John Porte's god-fathers, and was a trustee for two of Porte's sisters.

Porte's subsequent involvement with the syndicate which brought the first Curtiss F Flying Boat to England led to employment as test pilot to the White and Thompson Company, for which he worked until April 1914 when he left to join Curtiss for the Wanamaker Transatlantic flight attempt. The invitation had come from Glenn Curtiss who had been impressed by Porte's handling of the F Boat at Brighton. The flight was planned in the hope of winning the £10,000 ($US50,000) which had been offered by the *Daily Mail* for the first crossing of the Atlantic by a heavier-than-air machine. Rodman Wanamaker, the wealthy store owner, contributed $US25,000 to cover the cost of an aircraft to make the flight which was to commemorate the 100th anniversary of peace between the United States and Britain. For this reason, there had to be an American and a British pilot.

On its arrival, assembly and launching at Lake Keuka, the *America*, as the big flying boat had been named, was found to fly well in its unladen state, but refused to leave the water when loaded with 2,200 lbs of sand-bags which represented the estimated weight of fuel required for the Atlantic crossing. Although Porte had been employed mainly as a pilot, he very soon became fully occupied with the redesign of the hull and eventually at least 28 changes were made before *America* would take off with full load. These changes even included the fitting of a third engine above the upper wing. The final hull form incorporated sponsons on either side of the forebody of the hull to provide additional flotation and planing area. A second hull was built as a spare for the record attempt.

John Porte had an agreement with the Curtiss Company under which he was to receive 20% or 25% of any prize monies won, newspaper story rights and sales of all flying boats made by him. It would seem that this agreement had been negotiated with the assistance of Wanamaker's business manager Sumner R.Hollander, who was either offered, or assumed he would receive, a share of Porte's commissions. William Casson was to look after the interests of the project in Europe and to make any necessary disbursements there, in return for which he was to get a 50% share in the profits

accruing to Porte.

America was complete and in New York when war was declared in Europe on 4 August 1914. The Atlantic flight was immediately cancelled and John Porte sailed at once to England without, it is said, having time to pack all his belongings and to put his affairs in order. On his return, and in spite of his active tuberculosis, he immediately offered his services to the Admiralty and was appointed to command the R.N.A.S. Training School at Hendon with the rank of Squadron Commander.

On 13 August, Porte spoke to his old submarine chief, Captain Murray Sueter, who was, by now, Director of the Admiralty Air Department and gave him a glowing account of the potential value to the R.N.A.S. of the *America* flying boat. Porte followed this up with a letter dated 14 August which said:

Sir,
With reference to our conversation yesterday re the aeroplane "America" built by the Curtiss Aeroplane Company, I beg to forward herewith details and performances.

Motors:	*2 - 90 h.p. Curtiss (OX Type)*
Span:	*76 ft and 46 ft*
Chord:	*7 ft*
Gap:	*7 ft 6 ins*
Overall length:	*33 ft*
Surface:	*800 ft*
Weight:	*2,800 lbs*
Useful load:	*1,500 lbs (at least)*
Duration:	*20 hours (at least)*

The hull is built very strongly and should be capable of standing a good sea. She will arise from the water with great facility except when heavily loaded when it would be necessary to have a smooth sea. The machine is very steady in the air and specially built to facilitate navigation, the compass behaving well.

This machine should be finished this week, and I have no doubt it could be shipped next week.

A duplicate is about three parts built and could be shipped in about three weeks.

If it is desired, these machines could be purchased privately and shipped via Halifax, but there seems some doubt whether this course will be necessary.

The original price paid for these two Machines was £7,500 each but I am sure we could get them delivered in England for £6,000.

I understand you have a full record of the performance of this machine so I will not give any further details.

> *I have the honour to be, Sir,*
> *Your obedient Servant,*
> *J C PORTE*

After an exchange of cables, the purchase of *America* and her sister boat was agreed at £5,000 for one and £4,500 for the other on 29 August. The boats arrived in this country towards the end of October and were tested by Captain Sueter and Commander Porte. Following their favourable report, a further twelve boats of the *America* type were ordered on 31 October - four from Curtiss and eight to be built under licence by Aircraft Manufacturing Company. An order for spares for the first two *Americas* had already been placed on 17 October.

A soon as the first order had been confirmed by Curtiss, Casson realised that this and all subsequent purchases by the Admiralty would attract the 20-25% commission which had been promised to Porte and that for him to accept commission would be totally inconsistent with his position as a Royal Navy officer and agent of the Crown. Therefore a document was drawn up and signed by Casson and Porte as follows:

The British Deperdussin Aeroplane Company Ltd
Clun House, Surrey Street, W.C.

To: Mr. Wm A. Casson
Clun House, W.C.

My dear Casson,

The Admiralty having given me an appointment I must give up all my business connections but as these may be of some value I don't want simply to drop them and am willing to act on your suggestion and transfer everything to you to do your best with. Our partnership must come to an end so far as I am concerned and I therefore hereby transfer assign and make over absolutely to you all my interests in the Atlantic Flight, in the Curtiss Flying Boat and in my Contracts with Mr. Glenn Curtiss, the New York "World" and any others. The consideration for the foregoing assignment as between us is that you undertake to discharge all debts owing by me in connection with the Atlantic Flight and to proceed to America at your own expense if the business at any time demands it.

Faithfully yours,

(Sd) J.C.PORTE

I agree to the above,

(Sd) Wm A. Casson

In this, Porte purports to assign to Casson all his interests in the Atlantic Flight, the Curtiss Flying Boats and his contracts with the Curtiss Company. However, this document did not, as each of the signatories knew, truly set forth the real arrangement. There was a collateral verbal agreement that Casson should appear to be the person dealing with the Curtiss Company, that Porte's name should not appear and that of the profits accruing apparently to Casson, three-quarters would be handed to Porte and one-quarter retained by Casson. At no time did either Casson or Porte disclose to the Admiralty the financial interest they each had in the business with the Curtiss Company or that any commission was payable or was paid directly or indirectly to either of them.

On 10 November, Lyman J. Seeley returned to London to take up the position of European sales representative of the Curtiss Company and was immediately interviewed by Casson. Up to then, the arrangement with Porte had applied only to flying boats and possibly to engines used in them. Casson had realised that the R.N.A.S. was short of aircraft of all types and would need to buy whatever was readily available. An agreement was therefore made whereby Seeley would received his normal 1% commission on all Curtiss sales in Europe, plus an additional 15% on all sales made to the British Admiralty. Of this 15%, half was then transferred to Casson.

Up to September 1916, the amount of commission passed from Seeley to Casson was about £65,000. Of this, Casson retained a quarter and the remaining three-quarters, totalling about £48,000, was either paid directly to Porte, or in discharge of debts, in payment for motor cars or by investments in various securities.

In about August 1916, the Admiralty sent Lieutenant Neilson R.N.V.R. to America to investigate various matters concerning the working arrangements of the Curtiss Company in respect of their orders for the R.N.A.S. Whilst there, he saw Glenn Curtiss, amongst others, and heard rumours of commissions being paid to people in Britain in respect of Admiralty orders. It would seem possible that one source of such rumours may have been Sumner Hollander, who had been exchanging an acrimonious correspondence with Casson in an attempt to obtain payment of the share of commission which he felt was due to him from Porte.

Eventually Curtiss was forced to admit that, in addition to the 1% commission being paid to Seeley, they were paying 15% to "one Casson". This discovery was reported by Lieutenant Neilson and led to a revision of the contracts between the Admiralty and Curtiss as from September 1916 whereby all commissions were excluded and payment of them was discontinued.

Later in 1916, a Court of Inquiry was convened by the Admiralty to investigate the circumstances in which commission had been paid by Curtiss to persons in England on orders placed by the Admiralty. The investigation was held from January to May 1917 with Mr.J.G.Butcher K.C., M.P. presiding. Casson and Porte both gave evidence and produced all relevant documents which were still extant. Seeley, an American citizen, had already left the country and declined to make any written or verbal testimony.

The results of the enquiry were then sent to the Director of Public Prosecutions and a summons was issued on 24 July for Porte, Casson and Seeley to appear at Bow Street Police Court to answer charges that they had unlawfully and corruptly conspired together to contravene and set at naught the provisions of the Prevention of Corruption Act 1906 in respect of divers large sums of money received by John C.Porte, an agent of the Crown, in respect of certain contracts made between the Admiralty and the Curtiss Aeroplane Company of New York.

The hearing at Bow Street started on 3 August 1917 before Sir John Dickinson. The Attorney-General, Sir Frederick Smith, and Sir Archibald Bodkin appeared for the prosecution. Mr.W.J.Synott and Sir G.Lewis were the defending barristers. At the end of the first few day's hearings, Porte was taken ill with a severe haemorrhage and took no further part in the proceedings. The hearing lasted for over two weeks, at the end of which Casson and Porte were committed on bail for trial at the Central Criminal Court.

At the opening of the trial at the Old Bailey on 19 November, Casson pleaded guilty to twelve counts charging him with giving gifts to Porte, an agent of the Crown, as an inducement for showing favour to the Curtiss Aeroplane Company in relating to the business of the Crown. Mr.Justice McCardie fined Casson £6,000 and directed him to pay the costs of the prosecution. He was also obliged to return the remaining balance of commission received.

The Attorney-General then announced that in the case of Commander Porte he wished to enter a *Nolle Prosequi* and was withdrawing the charges against him. He then gave his reasons for this surprise action:

"At the outbreak of the war Commander Porte was in America occupying a commercial position in the aeronautic world which was a very advantageous one. Immediately on the outbreak of war he abandoned that position, came to England and placed his services unreservedly at the disposal of his country. At that time and now he was suffering from a most grave haemorrhage of the lung. At the present Commander Porte was doing invaluable work at the Admiralty in regard to the

national defence and the Admiralty were most anxious to retain his services. The progress of the malady from which he suffered was such that it was not possible to suppose that in any event the period for which his services would be at the disposal of his country would be a very protracted one. All the money paid to Porte, with the exception of £10,000, which had been disposed of, remained in his possession and the balance would be handed over by his representatives to the authorities."

Perhaps, because of the bad publicity and the effect on morale in the R.N.A.S., somebody in high places put the block on the prosecution and Porte went free, in spite of the volume of evidence which would surely have convicted a lesser man. However, the Crown received its "pound of flesh" as Porte had to agree to hand over to the Admiralty everything that remained of the commission that Curtiss had paid - about £30,000. It will be interesting to see in 1992, when the files from the Director of Public Prosecutions are made available at the Public Record Office, whether they cast any light on the decision not to proceed with the case against Porte.

Professor Sir Austin Robinson has recently summed up the case in the following words:

"I read avidly all that was published about the trial in the papers at the time. Before it came on, we all knew what was in the air and I remember discussions with others of my age and standing (other pilots on the F boats) in the mess at Felixstowe when I was there as a visiting ferry-pilot. We did not, of course, know all the evidence. But we knew enough to discuss seriously. The simple-minded way we looked at it was this: If Porte had not come back to fight and to command Felixstowe and had been content (or not required as an ex-Naval Officer) to remain a designer and developer of flying boats, in the same way that Sopwith, Fairey, Handley Page, A.V.Roe, Blackburn and De Havilland were, no-one would have objected to him being paid his profit or fee or whatever it might be. The Treasury or Air Board or Ministry of Munitions were there to see that it should not be too much. Porte's unforgivable crime was that he was not content to sit back and look on, but wanted to share in the fighting. To be respectable to the Treasury, one must not fight.

The great problem of aircraft design of 1914-1918 was the inadequacy of feed-back from operating experience to aircraft design. Any feed-back through the Air Board of the Admiralty was wholly inadequate. Very few people in the two headquarters had been on an operation of any sort for years past. The huge contribution of Porte was that he lived among pilots and was perpetually involved in the daily practical problems of operating and making not-so-good aircraft capable of operating. There was an instant and direct feedback. Thus the F boats were good, efficient working aircraft. Porte was in himself the instant feed-back. He not only tested the aircraft that he designed, he also flew them on long patrols. One was constantly wishing that one could have taken both the designers of the aircraft one had to fly and the senior officers in Whitehall who were buying them, on a long eight hour patrol. They might then have made them a lot more operable than they were.

What I am trying to say is that Porte's determination both to design and to fight was not only forgivable, it was also absolutely invaluable.

I can only go on to say that the effects of the Porte trial on morale were deplorable. Another light-hearted discussion at Felixstowe (out of hearing of our seniors) was concerned with the question of what target we would choose if we were bombed up and allowed to go anywhere. The unanimous choice was that we should destroy the "Bolo Hotel", which we believed to be the source of all our troubles.

At the time of the trial, John Porte was a very sick man and he knew himself that he was dying. He probably cared little about money and what the Treasury gnomes were arguing about. It was he who developed really operable flying boats and saw that they were built in Britain and not America. He was a great man, and the history of the War in the Air is right in saying so. "

Prior to his joining White & Thompson, Porte had no experience of the design and construction of flying boat hulls. However, he worked closely with Norman Thompson for some six months, during which time he was able to observe the inadequacy of the Curtiss F boats and the ways in which their hulls and flight organs were re-designed and reconstructed to make them seaworthy and airworthy. The experience and knowledge gained at Middleton enabled Porte to carry out most of the design work on the Curtiss *America*. The foundation of his flying skill on flying boats was also as a result of his time with White & Thompson.

An interesting feature of the whole sorry story is the ready acceptance by all concerned of the total disregard of the contract which had been negotiated between the Curtiss Company and White and Thompson and the way in which the British Government refused to allow Norman Thompson to sue the Curtiss Company for breach of contract.

The full transcript of the Court of Inquiry and subsequent trial is to be found in the Public Record Office (CRIM 1 File 169). Strangely, this is one of the few files, other than those relating to murder trials, which has survived from that era.

Early in 1917, Casson went to France on business and whilst there he seems to have had a presentiment that he might be torpedoed on the return crossing. He therefore drafted a fresh will and sent it to England, with a covering letter dated 12 February, from the Hotel Moderne at Le Havre. In the letter he made the following comments which are relevant to the corruption case:

Although the Bleriot Co. was a loss to me the Curtiss has succeeded and there are securities and monies in my safe so arranged as to explain the position. My Executor must hold certain of these in trust for Comr.J.C.Porte who will explain the position and point out what belongs to him. My property other than that which Porte is interested in is about £5,000 and as to the rest Porte is the real Owner of three fourths and I own one fourth and I hold everything in trust to be divided in this way. Commander Porte will claim what belongs to him and his word is to be accepted without question and acted upon.

No other person has any interest whatever in any property standing in my name but I have contracted with Edward Tilston to aid him with his engine and Mr.Wood of Wannamakers in Pall Mall East has an interest in that. If the engine is to do any good in the war it must be pushed at once. I have spent about £300 on the Patents and have agreed to go up to £2,500.

Moneys stand to my credit at Cox & Co, at Union London (Charing X) and at Farmers Loan and Trust Co Cockspur Street and also at New York. The Bank Accounts clearly shew what money is my own and what I hold as trustee for Porte. I have money also as trustee for Porte's sister being the balance of money her father gave her.

If I go to the bottom I do so feeling that I have tried to live a useful life and can end it with contentment. Prentice has got the blues at the idea of my making my Will but I do it as a precaution now that the Huns sink everything on sight.

Whilst accepting that John Porte was a sick man and filled with a single-minded purpose, that of designing and building war-winning flying boats, it is difficult to believe that he was so naive as to think that the acceptance of commission from a government contractor to a serving officer was normal conduct, especially in wartime. It is even more difficult to believe that he did not know that his previous employer, White & Thompson, held with the same contractor an *exclusive* agency for the introduction of their flying boats to the U.K. market, which introduction involved Porte himself flight testing the aircraft concerned for his then employers, White & Thompson. It seems probable that he was swayed by advice from Casson, a Svengali-like character who, as a barrister, should have known better!

CHAPTER 14

The Destruction of the Company

The whole sad story of the broken Curtiss agency agreement, the shabby, not to say dishonest, treatment of the Norman Thompson Company by the British Government and its eventual liquidation and takeover by the Handley Page Company makes disturbing reading and is best told in the words of Norman Thompson himself in a pamphlet which he wrote in December 1918:

INTRODUCTION

A dispassionate chronological record is set out below concerning the Government's treatment of The Norman Thompson Flight Co.Ltd. during the war, the accuracy of all statements therein being fully supported by available evidence.

The story is briefly this: For reasons which were partly brought to light by the Admiralty-Curtiss Corruption case in November 1917, the Admiralty ignored the Company at the beginning of the war as British Concessionaires for the Curtiss Aeroplane Co. U.S.A. and presumably came to regard them with disfavour. The Company had a very large claim against the Curtiss Co. for breach of agreement, and any procedure to recover this claim might lead to disclosures impugning the action of Government Officials.

Although the Government were approached in 1915 and 1916, their formal acquiescence to the Company taking steps to enforce their claim was extracted only in November, 1917, and subsequently the Minister of Munitions, Mr.Winston Churchill, personally intervened to refuse, without excuse or explanation, certain assistance to the Company in prosecuting their claim, which the Admiralty had agreed should be given.

As one of the earliest half-dozen experimental firms in this country and a pioneer in the development of the Flying Boat (see the opening paragraphs below) the Firm had more than ordinary right to expect just treatment, yet the Government finally brought them to ruin in April, 1918, by constantly keeping them short of orders, withholding payments overdue, and delaying settlement of claims, after encouraging them to undertake large extensions to their premises.

Having ruined the Firm the Government persistently refused to help them out of their difficulties, and finally prevented Mr.Thompson from recovering the position and business, which it had taken him nine years to build up, from the hands of the Receiver who had been put in by Messrs. Cox & Co., the Army Bankers as Debenture holders.

After placing considerable orders with the Receiver and paying up large arrears, which completely altered the Company's financial position, the action of the Aircraft Finance Department of the Ministry of Munitions practically forced the Company to transfer its business into the hands of Messrs. Cox & Co. under an agreement unwarrantably favourable to the latter. For they refused a request made to them by the Treasury to buy out Messrs. Cox & Co's debenture, expressly to prevent the agreement transferring the control of the Company to Messrs. Cox & Co. from going through, and so return the business into the hands of Mr.Norman Thompson and the original shareholders.

Thus the Government rewarded the Firm who introduced and developed the modern Flying Boat in Great Britain - a most important sea patrol and defence against U boats - by first forcing them to accept heavy losses, and then forcing their business out of their hands into those of other parties. No excuse or explanation for such treatment has ever been obtainable from the Government.

It will be noted from the following record that in some of their dealings the Admiralty, Air Ministry and Ministry of Munitions, showed a total disregard of the ordinary fair and straight dealing which used to be expected in this country.

THE NORMAN THOMPSON FLIGHT COMPANY LIMITED (Middleton, Bognor)

1. This firm devoted over 5 years to experimental work involving an outlay of some £18,000 from March, 1909, to August, 1914, and produced a few days before the outbreak of war the first British built Flying Boat of present day type - a machine of notable performance and sound construction which was immediately purchased by the Admiralty and used by the Navy.

2. This design by Mr.Norman Thompson, developed in structural details (type N.T.2B), was still being built for the Government by his Company at the date of the armistice, having been officially adopted by the Air Ministry in April, 1918, as their standard Naval instruction machine. Orders for this design were also placed by the Government with other Firms.

3. During the war the Company, a Controlled Firm, were engaged exclusively on aircraft work, and supplied to the Government large

and small Flying Boats of their own design, as well as a certain number of land machines.

4. In the winter of 1913-14 the Firm became interested in the original Curtiss Flying Boat from U.S.A., which Commander Porte, R.N., then the Company's pilot, tested at Bognor. Though ill impressed with its construction and flying capacity, Mr. Thompson subsequently acquired the exclusive rights for Curtiss Aircraft and Engines for a period of years from February 1st, 1914, as a policy of developing for his Firm, and with a view to designing and constructing Flying Boats in this country.

5. In the summer of 1915 the Admiralty Air Department asked for more production, which involved the Company in building considerable extensions to their Works. These were ready in May, 1916.

6. For the next 12 months after these extensions were completed the Company were only working at about one third full output owing to shortage of orders and constant changes in design, but the Admiralty refused to allow the War Office to place work with the Firm. During the last 8 months of 1916 not one machine could be completed for delivery.

7. In June 1917, the Air Board told the Company that they must further increase their production of Flying Boats and must again enlarge their Works, although the capacity of their existing Works had still been only partly utilised. The Company had spent all their money, had pledged their credit, and were claiming compensation for restriction of output. Until this compensation was paid, the Company's Balance Sheet showed a Loss which prevented further capital being found.

8. The Air Board therefore advanced £20,000 for new buildings which were designed specially for the production of one of the Company's designs of Flying Boat. At the same time in 1917, falling in with the views of the Government, the Company took over a small Works at Littlehampton for the immediate increase of the hull building capacity.

9. Suddenly without warning at the end of January, 1918, all orders for the particular Flying Boats, which the new buildings were expressly designed to accommodate, were cancelled, except as regards those already in hand, and, as had happened before, the Firm was brought up standing for want of work.

10. The Supply Department of the Air Ministry were anxious at once to substitute other orders, but did not possess the requisite powers to place contracts. Sundry interviews took place with different Officers of the Air Ministry up to the middle of April, but no new orders were forthcoming.

At a meeting towards the end of March, 1918, with the Air Ministry and several Head Officials, Mr. T.D. Nicol, the Director of Contracts Finance Department recommended the Government simply to cut their losses, referring to the money advanced by the Ministry of Munitions for the new buildings then approaching completion. He also complained, presumably by way of supporting his recommendation, that the Company had been badly managed, though no representation of the kind had ever been made to the Firm before. The Supply Department, who were alone competent to judge on such a matter, being in continuous touch with the Works, had, as Mr. Thompson subsequently ascertained, sent no report to this effect to Contacts Finance Department. The former Department had always realised the extreme difficulties thrown on the Firm by the withholding of orders.

Although previously urged by the Government to spend money on new buildings to increase production, and having been subsequently advanced £20,000 by the Government to further extend their works for the same object, the Company were now informed that their output, although useful, was not essential, but that, if they put their finances right (the state of which had been brought about by the action of the Government), then the Government would consider placing further orders.

11. The Company suggested that in the circumstances the Government should take over their Works, a proposal which was viewed favourably and as a just solution by the leading Supply Officials, but which was rejected by the Finance Department.

12. There was no complaint against the work turned out by the Company. The opinions expressed by Government Officials were invariably complimentary both as to workmanship and design.

13. The Company had had constant difficulty in obtaining payments from the Government, often long overdue, for work executed, and large sums were owing at that time. A settlement of the claim for compensation, referred to above, which was formally submitted in August, 1917, for transfer to the Lubbock Committee of the Treasury, had been constantly pressed for in vain.

On November 19th, 1917, a Director of the Company saw Mr. Nicol, the Director of Contracts Finance, who informed him that the claim was in the hands of the Treasury, and in answer to a further enquiry wrote a letter to this effect on January 24th, 1918. On February 13th, 1918, in answer to another enquiry Mr.Nicol's private Secretary informed this Director of the Company that the claim was in the Claims Department of the Ministry of Munitions. Mr.Thompson thereupon called on the latter department, and was informed that the documents of the claim had been received several months ago, but that intimation had only recently been received that the matter was urgent, and contrary to Mr.Nicol's statements the claim had never been submitted to the Treasury.

On March 26th, 1918, Mr.Nicol told the Director of the Company alluded to above that the Lubbock Committee had definitely turned down the claim. Mr.Thompson thereupon applied to the Claims Department for confirmation of the fact which was absolutely denied. The Committee merely required more information before reaching any decision.

A decision by the Ministry of Munitions was still outstanding as to the amounts of royalties due on one of the Company's designs of Flying Boat for which the Ministry had placed orders with other Firms, though the subject had been under consideration since September, 1917.

14. Under these circumstances with considerable justification Messrs. Cox & Co., the Army Bankers, who held a debenture of £30,000 from the Company put in a Receiver on April 19th, 1918. The Government had been informed that such action was contemplated, and up to the last moment certain Officials tried in vain to get sufficient arrears paid up by the Company, and so forestall the event.

15. Sundry interviews then took place between Messrs. Cox & Co. and the Ministry of Munitions, and finally in May a small repeat order of N.T.2B Flying Boats, representing about six weeks work for the factory, was placed with the Receiver. Subsequently at the beginning of August a further order was placed for machines of the same design with spares, representing work for six months or so.

16. Shortly after the appointment of the Receiver, Messrs. Cox & Co. proposed a re-arrangement of the Company's Capital under which they would find £15,000 against Prior Lien Debentures, if the existing shareholders would surrender to them the majority of their shares; and certain terms were offered to the ordinary creditors. The Company's financial position and outlook for future orders having been so heavily prejudiced by the Government's action the shareholders were unable to put forward any alternative scheme, and therefore felt bound not to oppose Messrs. Cox &

Co.'s proposals if the ordinary creditors wished to accept them, a decision which they eventually reached.

17. On July 20th the following letter was sent to the Air Minister, Lord Weir, who had for some time been fully acquainted with the treatment of the Company both at the hands of the Admiralty and the Air Board. The summary referred to in the letter gave generally the facts stated above and those hereafter, relating to the Curtiss Co., U.S.A.

July 29th, 1918

The Lord Weir
Air Minister
Hotel Cecil
London

My Lord,

Referring to the various interviews which I and other representatives of my Company had had with various Officials of the Air Ministry during the last six months since the sudden cancellation of orders on January 25th of this year, I enclose a Summary showing the treatment my Firm has experienced at the hands of the Government.

The clear result has been the ruin of my Company. It will be at once clear to you that such treatment is contrary to national and public interest, and on this ground I make a last formal appeal to have the situation rectified as far as may be possible at this late hour.

Immediate action will be necessary, for the patience of the staff which has been excellent under most trying conditions has naturally come to an end.

I have been constantly assured by certain Officials that the output of the Firm is essential, yet no decision has been reached today by the Government with regard to future orders or carrying on the business.

The least the Government can do as a matter of justice is to take over the Works from the Company on a fair basis, and pay up all back claims, at the same time taking over the debenture from the Bank, who only advanced money to the Company assuming the Firm would be normally treated.

I am, my Lord,
Your obedient Servant

THE NORMAN THOMPSON FLIGHT CO
Norman A. Thompson
Managing Director

An immediate acknowledgment was received from the Air Minister explaining that he had handed the letter to Sir Arthur Duckham, the Director

General of Aircraft Supplies, to deal with, as it related to matter of Aircraft production. No further reply or acknowledgement whatever has yet been received.

18. On August the 7th, 1918, Mr.Joynson-Hicks, Chairman of the Parliamentary Air Committee, asked a series of questions in the House of Commons on the points dealt with above, and received a written reply from the Parliamentary Secretary to the Minister of Munitions, Mr.Kellaway. The answers were such as to shed no light on the real state of affairs.

19. Late in September, 1918, a representative of the Lubbock Committee of the Treasury, to whom the Company's claim for loss of production in 1916 had been referred, asked Mr.Thompson to call on him. He pointed out that, as the Minister of Munitions had recently paid up the greater portion of its arrears and placed further considerable orders with the Company, it should not now be difficult for the Firm to find someone to buy out Messrs. Cox & Co's debenture and to obtain any further capital required on reasonable terms, for the conditions which Messrs. Cox & Co. sought to impose were wholly unwarranted. These involved control of all the assets, including a claim of some hundreds of thousands of pounds against the Curtiss Co., U.S.A., standing since 1916, and a major share of all profits, for undertaking to advance up to a further £15,000 against Prior Lien Debentures, subject to the Firm continuing to obtain profitable orders from the Government, and with the right to call in their Debentures at any time at one month's notice.

In view of the probable approach of peace, Mr.Thompson found it impracticable at the last moment to obtain the necessary financial assistance to purchase Messrs. Cox & Co's interest.

20. On October 8th the Lubbock Committee, before deciding as to any payment in respect of the Company's claim, recommended that the Ministry of Munitions should purchase Messrs. Cox & Co's debenture so that the control of the Company should be given back to Mr.Thompson and the original shareholders. The Aircraft Finance Department refused to entertain this suggestion, thus supporting the terms of Messrs. Cox & Co's scheme of re-arrangement, which the Company were finally forced to accept.

21. On December 2nd, the Lubbock Committee finally decided against any allowance on the claim either to the existing Company or Mr.Thompson personally. With sympathy for Mr.Thompson and the original shareholders in the heavy losses imposed on them they had considered the possibility of allowing some compensation to Mr.Thompson personally, but after taking legal advice came to the decision above.

22. The Company as sole concessionaire for Curtiss Aircraft and Engines for a period of years from February 1st, 1914, have a claim against the Curtiss Aeroplane Company of U.S.A. amounting to hundreds of thousands of pounds for breach of Agreement in respect of large orders placed direct with them by the Admiralty during the first two years of the War.

23. The possession by the Company of the Curtiss Rights in Great Britain, though it had been regularly shown on their letter paper and in their trade advertisements, was persistently ignored by the Admiralty from the beginning of the War. The placing of contracts with the Curtiss Company was at first entirely unknown to Mr.Thompson's Company.

24. On January 7th and three subsequent dates in the early part of 1915 the Company wrote to the Secretary of the Admiralty, Sir Graham Greene, asking for an explanation, but no answer to these letters were ever received beyond an acknowledgment of receipt of the first. Evidence of the remaining three letters having reached the Admiralty transpired when Mr.Thompson was examined in January, 1917, by Sir John Butcher, K.C. during the private enquiry regarding the illicit commissions paid by the Curtiss Company.

On February 3rd, 1915, the Curtiss Company wrote attempting to repudiate their agreement with Mr.Thompson's Company.

25. Having been refused permission hitherto by the Admiralty to press their claim, the Company wrote to Sir Eric Geddes on August 10th, 1917, who replied suggesting that Mr.Thompson should see Sir Oswyn Murray, the Secretary of the Admiralty. Mr.Thompson therefore had an interview with Sir Oswyn Murray on October 3rd, 1917, who stated that he saw no objection to the Company taking action at once against the Curtiss Company nor to their being given particulars of the Contracts placed by the Admiralty with the Curtiss Company, and that he would see Sir William Weir on the subject. In fact Sir Oswyn Murray offered every assistance that could be expected.

In a letter dated November 7th, 1917, from Mr.T.D.Nicol, Director of Aeronautical Contracts, the Company received formal permission to press their claims against the Curtiss Company.

26. On January 7th, 1918, in view of steps to recover their claim the Company wrote to Sir William Weir asking for the particulars of the

Curtiss Contracts, which Sir Oswyn Murray saw no objection to handing to the Company, but a reply came, dated March 11th, 1918, from Mr. Winston Churchill, the Minister of Munitions, through his private secretary, refusing the information without offering any explanation.

Thus once more the Company were met with obstruction instead of assistance by the Government in seeking to recover a very large sum of money in which the Treasury was heavily interested in virtue of Excess Profits Duty. Owing to the financial straits to which the Company had been reduced, the prosecution of the claim is still in abeyance.

27. It is almost unnecessary to state that the incomprehensible treatment of the Company recorded above severely hampered production, tended to dishearten employees, and threw continuous and, at times, insuperable difficulties on the staff and management. Development of manufacturing facilities and conditions of comfort for employees were alike impeded, and the organisation was frequently dislocated.

28. The only explanation behind the facts set out in this statement appears to be that the Government in certain influential quarters came to regard the Company with disfavour simply because they happened to be owners of the Curtiss rights, and feared disclosures against themselves, if the Company sought redress from the Curtiss Company for breach of contract.

The above suggestion derives support from the abrupt close of the Curtiss Corruption case in the Criminal Court in November, 1917, when according to reports in the Press, the Attorney General, Sir F.E.Smith, entered a "nolle prosequi" after the prisoners were found guilty, and they were set free on handing back what they still possessed of the £48,000 of which they were held to have defrauded the Admiralty.

The undersigned was informed by a competent authority that his Firm's position in regard to the Curtiss rights prejudiced the settlement of the Firm's claim for loss of production. Yet the two matters were absolutely distinct and unconnected.

29. In view of the abnormal judicial procedure just cited, the Company have had little confidence in recourse to the law for redress in any respect from the Government.

Norman A. Thompson
Late Managing Director
The Norman Thompson Flight Co. Ltd.
Middleton, Bognor

Cox & Co., the bankers, were appointed Receivers and Managers on 19 April 1918 and their representatives A.W.Haschke and Ernest Cameron joined the Board. Norman Thompson thereupon resigned. Frederick Handley Page was given a portion of the shares surrendered by old shareholders to Cox & Co. and was induced to join the board so as to bring orders to the Company. The Handley Page Company started to expand after the end of the war and in July 1919 bought the Norman Thompson factories and stock from the liquidators. The proceeds were used to satisfy part of the liabilities and the Company went into voluntary liquidation on 12 July 1919. The Receivers had reported "the works are some six or seven miles from Bognor and there are practically no transport facilities. The new buildings, erected at the command of the Government, have never been used. Owing to the cessation of hostilities there is a great drop in the value of aeroplane stocks and the Company has much material on hand which it is feared would not realise much at break-up prices. Nevertheless there is a surplus of £27,837 available for distribution among Debenture holders subject to the expenses of liquidation."

Frederick Handley Page himself went to America in an apparently fruitless attempt to persuade the Curtiss Company to settle the outstanding claim by the Norman Thompson Company for breach of their agency agreement. The Handley Page Company tried hard to open up a market for small flying boats and his Aircraft Disposal Company offered N.T.2Bs complete with new Wolseley Viper engines for £1,100. Only one came on the British Civil register, but several were sold abroad - to Canada, Norway, Peru, China and Estonia; the remainder must have quickly been disposed of as scrap. Handley Page had claimed that all drawings and designs were included in his purchase and they were transferred from Middleton to Cricklewood; however, in 1922 they were partly given up and returned to the liquidators.

Norman Thompson's bitterness remained with him all his life and in his will he directed that his remains should not repose in Great Britain, still less in the U.S.A., for the reason that "since ascertaining by experience gained during the war of 1914-1918 that England had allowed herself to come under the rule of corruption and intrigue directed by hidden alien forces, my otherwise natural feelings of personal allegiance towards that country have ceased to exist".

In 1923, the liquidators attempted to obtain royalties from the Government for the 64 N.T.2Bs which were built by Saunders and Supermarine, but once again they were turned down.

However, Norman Thompson eventually received a measure of recognition for his work for the country during World War One when the Royal Commission on Awards to Inventors recognised him as the one designer who had contributed to the development of the flying boat in the 1914/18 war and awarded the liquidators £2,250 which was eventually passed on to him. In 1927 he was given a further personal award of £3,000.

He must have been particularly satisfied when the Commission turned down applications from Glenn Curtiss and Mrs. Minnie Porte (John Porte's widow). Mrs. Porte was eventually awarded £1,500 by the U.S. Government in recognition of her husband's services to America.

The invention for which Norman Thompson claimed had been notified originally to the Admiralty in July 1914 and covered the principle of a tailplane negatively inclined to the slipstream to neutralise the nose-diving couple produced by the propeller thrust and combined with a centre of gravity forward of the centre of pressure. He claimed that his invention had been used on some 324 flying boats produced during the war. Taking an average value of £5,000 apiece and a one percent royalty, this would have given Thompson £16,200.

It is interesting to note the similarities in the treatment of the Norman Thompson Company and the way in which the British Government attempted to gain control of the Hendon Aerodrome from Claude Grahame-White at the end of the War at a fraction of its true worth. The shady tactics were much the same in both cases. However, Grahame-White had some powerful and wealthy relatives and friends and eventually won his rightful compensation. Poor Norman Thompson had no such useful allies and his company went to the wall.

Aerial view of the New City Holiday Camp occupying the Norman Thompson factory buildings from July 1922

CHAPTER 15 - ENVOI

As related earlier, the Handley Page Company bought most of the assets of the Norman Thompson Company from the Liquidator at the beginning of 1919 and these included most of the freehold land (about 7½ acres) and the buildings thereon. Handley Page had set up the Flying Boat Company Ltd. with a view to operating passenger flights from the South Coast and some of the surplus N.T.2Bs and N.T.4as were converted at Middleton for potential civil use. It has been reported that some of these machines were flown to Hendon, where they landed on the Welsh Harp reservoir and were then offered for sale by the Aircraft Disposal Company. However, by the end of 1919 it was apparent that the sales potential for this type of aircraft was very limited and Handley Page decided to get rid of the South Coast "albatross".

The 7½ acres, together with buildings, plant, machinery, vehicles and boats, were put up for auction at Middleton on 17/24 February 1920, the auctioneers being Hall, Pain and Goldsmith of Portsmouth. At the same time, another approximately 2 ½ acres, with buildings, were auctioned on behalf of the Liquidator.

The site and building appear to have been bought by a company which demolished some of the buildings and converted others for use as a holiday camp, one of the first to appear in Britain, and this duly opened in July 1922 as "The New City Holiday

Camp". It closed in the autumn and re-opened for its first full season on 1 May 1923. Once of the large hangars was sold to Bognor Council, dismantled and re-erected near the sea front in Waterloo Square as "The Pavilion". It was used as a theatre and dance hall until 1948 when it was demolished following a fire. The holiday camp was at some stage renamed "South Dene Holiday Camp" and following World War Two it became the "Sussex Coast Country Club". It is now owned by Ladbrokes Ltd.

At the present time the remaining large hangar and seven erecting shops (a group of three and a group of four) are still clearly recognisable. The sea wall has been considerably strengthened, but there are still traces of the slipway.

Norman Thompson's home "Ancton House" still remains.

It is still possible to trace some remains of Hubert Williams' "Britannia Works" at Fisherman's Quay, Littlehampton.

Apart from the TNT propeller in Bromley and a N.T.2B propeller in the Tangmere Museum, the only other known Norman Thompson aircraft relics are in the care of the Humberside Aircraft Preservation Society at Cleethorpes.

Not a great memorial to a patriotic enterprise murdered by British bureaucracy and the "Establishment".

APPENDIX I

Lanchester and his Aeronautical Patents

Frederick Lanchester's first two applications for aeronautical patents (No.3538 of 1893 and 12744 of 1896) were abandoned and unfortunately details of these have not survived. Equally unfortunately, his paper given before the Birmingham Natural History and Philosophical Society in June 1894 and entitled *The Soaring of Birds and the possibilities of Mechanical Flight* was never published and details of it have been lost. However, it seems to have been well received by the distinguished gathering and, in 1897, he filed his first successful aeronautical patent (No.3608).

This patent shows a sophisticated, streamlined monoplane, with high aspect ratio wings, which was light years ahead of the Wright Brothers' primitive biplanes five years later. Lanchester's ideal was summed up in his comment: "In constructing a machine in accordance with the present invention I arrange a body of elongated and preferable streamline form of suitable dimensions to contain the propelling and other mechanisms and to provide suitable accommodation for whatever purpose required. The form of wing to support the weight of the machine is preferably that of the soaring bird, that is to say of great lateral breadth and small for and aft dimensions. The plan-form is preferably elliptical. The tailplane acting in conjunction with the supporting wings has for its principal functions the preservation of longitudinal equilibrium and the regulation of speed, whilst the fins are concerned with maintenance of transverse equilibrium and control of geographic direction, the inclination of the course to the horizontal is under the control of the propeller thrust."

The aeroplane that was eventually built, the Thompson Lanchester No.1, although a biplane, incorporated many of the features of the monoplane described in the patent twelve years previously.

Lanchester subsequently filed the following patents covering aeroplanes, aero engines, propellers, etc. but never again designed an aeroplane which was actually built:

Year	Patent No.	Title
1893	3538	Aerial Machines. Abandoned
1896	12744	Aerial Machines. Abandoned
1897	3608	Aerial Machines
1905	17935	Aerodromes
1907	9413	Aerodromes
1907	9413A	Propeller driving mechanism
1908	18065	Imparting stability to aerodrome in flight. Abandoned
1909	8849	Steering flying-machines etc.
1909	10422	Flying-machines
1909	18303	Aeronautical machines. Aband.
1909	18384	Flying-machines
1910	5676	Aerial Machines. Abandoned
1911	9873	Aeronautical machine engines
1911	21360	Aeronautical machines
1911	22502	Aeronautical machines. Aband.
1911	23271	Flying machines
1914	17546	Radial engines
1914	17775	Aeronautical engines
1919	127620	Mechanism for receiving and launching aeroplanes at sea
1919	129727	Lateral plumb indicator for aircraft
1919	130025	Attachment of aeronautical propellers
1919	130070	Aeroplanes

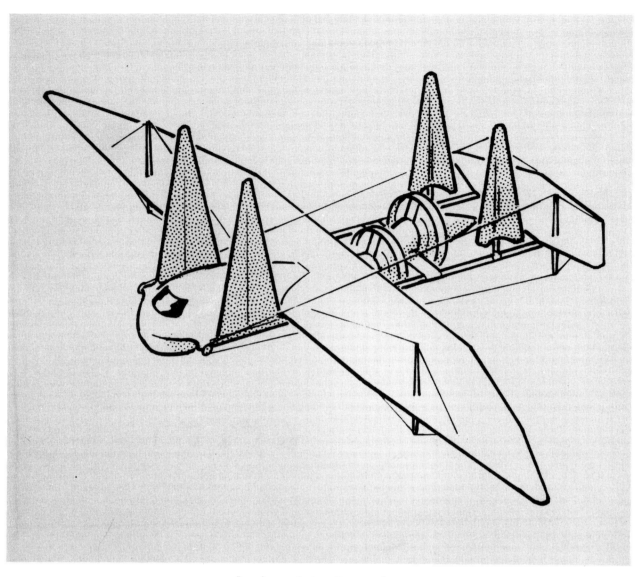

Lanchester designs for aeroplanes

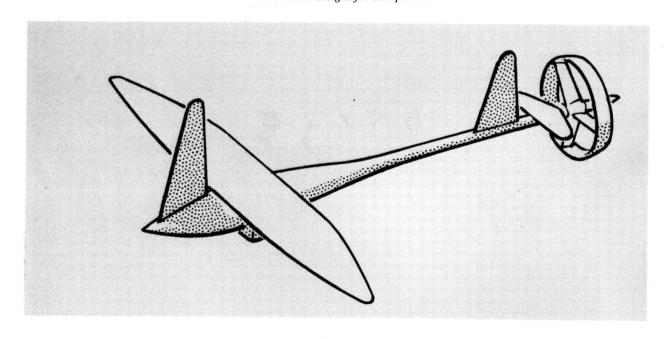

APPENDIX II

S.E. Saunders Ltd. and their Consuta Plywood

Moses Saunders opened a boat-building business in 1830 at Streatley-on-Thames and he subsequently moved his yard to Goring-on-Thames where boats up to 85 tons displacement were built.

Samuel E. Saunders, the founder's grandson, took control of the company towards the end of the nineteenth century. He was greatly interested in marine racing craft and yachts and decided that there would be more future for the company if they moved to Cowes which, by then, was the premier centre in Britain and perhaps the world, for national and international yacht racing and sporting events. He initially moved to a small yard in West Cowes in 1901 but very soon transferred to larger premises on the other side of the River Medina at East Cowes. Within a short space of time they were building a large variety of sailing boats and motorised yachts and had started designing a range of very fast launches.

Traditionally, boat hulls were planked with strips of mahogany and other hard woods, either with a smooth finish or with overlapping (clinker-built) planks. In an effort to improve the strength to weight ratio, to produce a smoother finish and to speed up production, trials were made with the relatively new multi-plywood sheets. However, at that time synthetic waterproof glues were not available and animal glues deteriorated quickly if they were affected by damp for any length of time.

Varnished or painted hulls were satisfactory at first but eventually the protective coating would give way, the wood became sodden, the glue lost its adhesive qualities and the ply layers opened up.

The solution was clever and relatively simple and was patented in 1898 by "Sammy" Saunders (Patent No.222). The layers of thin wood were glued and then sewn together with waxed thread or copper wire. Refinements to the invention were patented in 1909 (No.23333) and 1912 (No.3640). The sewn plywood was given the trade name "Consuta".

Racing hydroplanes were built from 1908 onwards, the hulls of which were clad with Consuta ply and shortly afterwards a department was set up to construct seaplanes, flying boats and landplanes, many of which were partly built of Consuta.

A new factory was built upstream from Cowes at Whippingham, next to the Folly Inn, and this was used for the large-scale production of Consuta ply. Giant sewing machines were installed in this factory and vast quantities of plywood were produced between 1900 and about 1950. During World War One alone, 100,000 super feet of Consuta was produced at the Folly Works.

The original motor launch named *Consuta*, built by Saunders and used eventually as a stake boat in the Oxford and Cambridge Boat Race, is now on show at the Steam Engine Museum at Kew Bridge.

APPENDIX III

F. P. H. Beadle - the Designer

In 1913, Percy Hyde Beadle joined E.W. Copeland Perry, a pilot who trained with Sopwith at Brooklands, and set up a company, Perry, Beadle and Company, at Twickenham to manufacture aircraft. During its brief existence, Beadle designed several machines of various types, only two of which seem actually to have been built. One was a small two-seater biplane, the other a single-engined flying boat of novel design.

On the outbreak of war in August 1914, Perry joined the R.F.C. as a pilot and the Company closed down. Beadle went to White and Thompson as chief designer and assistant to Norman Thompson.

Following the unsuccessful official trials of the T.N.T. flying boat, Beadle left Norman Thompson and joined the newly-formed Gosport Aircraft Company as chief designer. His assistant was R.J. Ashfield who had recently been virtually forced out of his job at Sopwith when W.G. Carter had taken over much of his design responsibility.

After leaving Gosport when their ambitious plans for very large civil flying boats proved to be financially unrealistic, Percy Beadle went to S.E. Saunders Ltd. in November 1919, together with his chief draughtsman from his Norman Thompson days, H.W. Gravenell. Together they designed the Kittiwake twin-engined amphibian, to be entered for a Government-sponsored competition for civil aviation held in August 1920. Unfortunately the Kittiwake was not completed in time and when it was eventually flight-tested its novel form of wing construction gave rise to a partial collapse of the wing and a hurried landing. The design was not developed. Beadle designed a seaplane for the 1927 Schneider Trophy race, similar in appearance to the Supermarine S.5, but it was not built due to lack of financial support. In addition to his work on aircraft, he also became involved in the hull design of power boats and, following the disappointing performance of the large four-engined boat built for Betty Carstairs for an attempt on the Atlantic record, he left Saunders and subsequently went to the U.S.A. in 1929 at the request of Fairchild Aircraft to take charge of their float design team. When Fairchild opened their plant in Canada, Beadle went to them in February 1931 as Chief Engineer. Whilst there. he designed floats for De Havilland Canada as well as for Fairchild. In 1936 he left Fairchild and was succeeded by N.F. Vanderlepp, formerly of Bellanca. Beadle then went to the newly-formed Aircraft Division of the National Steel Car Company of Malton, Ontario, as Chief Engineer. In 1938 he was sent to Westland at Yeovil to look at Lysander production, for which N.S.C.C. subsequently obtained a licence. The first Canadian-built Lysander flew in August 1939.

In 1941, he went to De Havilland Canada as Chief Engineer and, in 1942, he transferred to Central Aircraft Ltd., London, Ontario, as Chief Engineer and General Manager. He died there on 14 December 1943.

APPENDIX IV

Norman Thompson and White & Thompson Patents

1911

1605	Framework of aeroplanes etc.
11733	Aeroplane and etc. motors Abandoned
19665	Aeroplane etc. Safety harness releases
20030	Control of flying machines. Abandoned

1912

6460	Spring arrangements
6461	Flying Machine running gear
7174	Flying Machines etc. Abandoned
12655	Aeroplanes (drive extensions)
21604	Aeroplanes etc. structures (metal wings)
23744	Flying Machines etc. running gear
28205	Propellers

1913

1909	Aircraft (metal wings)
2893	Helmets etc. Abandoned
3733	Wheel construction
6869	Airships
12641	Propellers. Abandoned

1918

117309	Launching and landing of Aircraft

1920

146681	Alighting gear for Aircraft (floats)

Below left: Patent suspension of fuselage of Norman Thompson No. 1 Biplane

Below right: Patent variable pitch propeller

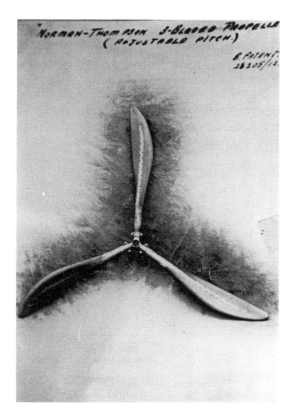

APPENDIX V

The Directors of the Company

1912

Arthur Norman	Chairman
Norman Arthur Thompson	Managing Director
John Douglas Campbell White	
Charles Wolrycle Dixon	
Arthur Bonsor	

1917

Arthur Thompson	Chairman
Norman Arthur Thompson	Managing Director
Lewis Norman Way	Secretary
Rupert Spens Thompson	
Robert William Armstrong Gilfillan	
Lee Murray	
William James Thompson	

April 1917

Robert W.A. Gilfillan
Albert William Haschke
Ernest Cameron
F. Handley Page
F.A. Smalley

APPENDIX VI

Some Members of the Staff of the Company

Mr.N.M. Hiskins	General Manager. Succeeded by Mr.S. Dickinson	Mr. Sutton	Boat Shop
Mr.Rounthwaite	Works Manager	Mr.E. Robinson	Fitter
Mr.Dodds	Office Manager	Mr.J. Perry	Tool Room
Lieut. McCann R.N.	Admiralty Representative	Mrs. Sharpe	Carpenters' Shop
Mr.F.P.H. Beadle	Chief Designer	Mr. Dowland	Erectors' Shop
Mr.A. Bedford	Chief Draughtsman	Miss Clemisha	Welfare - Canteen Manageress
Mr.Kerr	Head Draughtsman		
Mr.H.W. Gravenell	Drawing Office	Mr. Harvey	
Mr.T.M. Camp	Drawing Office	Mr. Brown	
Mr. Roberts	Drawing Office	Mr.H. Pettit	
Mr.A. Carmichael	Drawing Office	Mr.G. Hartley	
Mr.F. Brown	Drawing Office	Mr.G. Wright	
Mrs. Cicely Holmes	Tracer	Mr.E. Brackley	
Mrs. E.W. Roberts	Purchasing	Mr.R. Terry	
Mr. Singleton	Welfare	Mr. de Florac	
Miss V.M. Donaldson	Stores	Mr. Harrower	Inspector
Mr. Powell	Erecting Shop Foreman	Mr. Ragless	
Mr.G. Sims	Chargehand in Erecting Shop	Mr. Rawlings	
Mr. Fred Williams	Foreman Boat-builder	Dr. Blunt	Company Doctor
Mr.P.H. Bailey	Chargehand	Mr. Fred Newland	A.I.D. Inspector in Erecting Shop
Mr.G.C. King	Works Department		Dope Shop
Mrs.E. Mitchell	Works Department	Mr.G. Horner	
		Mr.A. Richards	
		Mr. Blogg	

APPENDIX VII

Letter from Norman Thompson to Frederick Lanchester

c/o Lloyds Bank
43 Bd des Capucines
Paris
4.6.37

My dear Lanchester,

I have at last had a moment to consider the further information you asked for re our first machine, but only with unsatisfactory results. All records of trials were scooped or destroyed when Handley Page took hold of the works under the receiver. I should place the date of the first trial towards the end of 1910. After the meeting at Rheims in the summer of 1909 we began work at Daimler in the autumn of that year, and I first received the machine (bodywork with engines mounted) at Bognor in the spring of 1910, where I had to make the flight organs. Most of 1911 was spent in trials and modifications; early 1912 it was finally scrapped, White was not ready to continue finding money and was in a state of general hesitation, you then withdrew formally from your position as advisory engineer to the Company, and I designed a machine of more ample wing surface with a piano wire wing construction, sheet steel body carrying an "A.B.C." 120 H.P. engine in front with a pusher propeller, and with the normal amount of sundry freakisms that need not be mentioned. The machine was tested by a very good pilot, E.R. Whitehouse, summer 1913; he liked it on its first trials, and it flew a short stretch quite well over the Ancton sands, but a couple of months later, when it had been refitted, Porte, who had just come to me as the firm's permanent pilot, piled it up badly on a patch of rocks on the sand before making an attempt to get off. As I had already decided to concentrate on the development of the flying boat (Autumn 1913), we had not time or money to rebuild the pusher aeroplane referred to above.

I then became interested in the Curtiss Flying boat, which Curtiss was showing off in England during that winter. Porte flew it several times, and finally on Feb. 1st 1914 I signed an agreement for my firm of White & Thompson Ltd with the Curtiss Co for a 12 years exclusive agency for G.B. & Dominions for their aircraft (I believe aeroplanes were included as well as their flying boats) and engines. On the delivery of the Curtiss flying boat under the above agreement at our works Porte carried out tests, which revealed such criminal defects and generally poor construction throughout that these boats were unfit for sale, and I decided in March or April 1914 to design a completely independent model of flying boat myself. The rest of the story you know. I knew then from experience the danger in flying a flying boat when cutting in or cutting out the engine; and I knew since reading your 2 volumes in 1908 the undesirability of putting positive load on the tail. Exactly when it struck me first that a slight "negative" load on the tail would obviously solve the problem I cannot say - probably a little later on in the summer, when I remember getting out personally 3 charts as usual of the weights of all the detail parts in order to obtain the C.G. in the 3 views, and study the weight distribution, after getting most of the necessary information from Kerr, my head draughtsman at that time. These sheets with other personal calculations were kept in a folder in my desk, which I could not find at the time of the receiver's installation when clearing out my desk.

As to my crash in your first machine I have nothing to add to what I told you the other day. I was just about getting up to speed on the sand with the engines all out, when the two right wheels buckled and the machine turned upside down directly over its nose. I had no sensation of alarm or discomfort, but crept out and sent for the photographer.

Wilmot Nicholson has no photo of this machine except a duplicate of the one you have without wings on - this I have at present as it is a better print.

In regard to the N.T.2 flying boat, which I completed before the war and before I had anyone capable of designing on the place but myself, you have one or two careful descriptions of its features in the papers I sent you.

I saw Miss Douglas-Pennant before I left London. She particularly appreciated your message to her, which I delivered, that you would be prepared to give her information, if desired, which might assist her. Having a watchful eye on subterranean politics she attended both my patent claims, remembers you very well and quoted certain things you said, which I had forgotten!

It was very nice seeing you again and your wife - I wish it had been longer and that we could have had more time for a chat on the way the world goes.

Yours always faithfully

Norman A Thompson (sg)

Addenda on 5.6.37

Dear Lanchester

I note a mental aberration in mine of yesterday.

The aereoplane I built in 1912 had a <u>pusher</u> propeller, but the engine was in front with the radiator. A propeller shaft conected the two lying along the floor centrally. The steel body allowed a nice fixing for the propeller and thrust bearing; there was an universal joint of course next the rear of the engine. The pilots of that date appreciated this combinationof a free view in front without a prospect of the engine on top of them in a crash.

I fancy you have a photo of the above freak effort.

So long, yrs always sincerely

NAT

APPENDIX VIII

Copy of letter from Dr. Douglas White, dated 30.9.37 to Dr. F.W. Lanchester

Dear Lanchester,

I was glad to get your letter this morning. Referring to what you say of my attitude towards the original venture and the reasons why I fell out of it later, your ideas in general are right, though not as to the cause of my breaking with Mr. Thompson.

I started the experimental factory mainly out of patriotic motives, as N.A.T. explained to me how far behind the country was in flying machines. Partly also out of personal interest in the progress of aviation. It is true that the progress of things consumed considerably more money than I thought it would. You may remember that we bought the rights for this country of the Curtiss Flying Boats, I think in 1913. Porte was with us and learnt with us all he knew about flying. The first flying boat was ready for the Daily Mail £10,000 Round England Flights (it was to have been through the Caledonian Canal) before Aug. 1st 1914 which was the date of the race. It was of course put off owing to the war - expectation - and on Aug.5th the Admiralty commandeered it and took it away to Felixstowe (picture in book) where I was told it was the only sea-plane there which could be trusted to fly when wanted in the first year of the war!

We then built six more for the Admiralty; but N.A.T. had a nervous breakdown in October of that year and had to go away to Egypt. I remained in control and ran the concern for some 7 months till June 1915, having Dodds as office manager and Rounthwaite as works-manager. We came to the conclusion that we could not expand at Ancton into an extensive factory, but failed after some hunting to find a suitable place. In June 1915 N.A.T. returned in better health; he thought we could expand at the same place. I could not agree. He was backed by his father who bought me out at a low figure, and enabled N.A.T. to build more sheds. I left, and joined the R.A.M.C. which, after all, was my proper job (and I hope did quite useful work in the war). N.A.T. then built a large number of aeroplanes; what then happened I only know by hearsay: viz: that he was for some reason unpopular at the Admiralty, and he became stacked up with aeroplanes for which he could not get engines, and so the whole thing came to grief. It was a wretched story. Perhaps the business got into the hands of a small ring of commercial firms.

During the 7 months when I had control we made 6 more flying boats and a considerable number of land machines. The first of the six boats I delivered to Dover in February 1915, taking Gordon England as pilot. That was an exciting day. It was the first seaplane at Dover during the war. All Dover was out to see us arrive. I was almost stone deaf for two days after.

So, you see, it was not merely the money question that frightened me, but a difference of opinion between N.A.T. and myself. In any case it was not my job in the war.

I never expected any return on money expended. I just felt that the country needed work done on flying and though I could help in company with N.A.T.

I think I have answered your questions. I dropped a good deal of money over the thing but my son told me he thought it was the only thing I had ever done that was worth doing; and it is a matter of some satisfaction that I was an agent in building the first flying boat in this country - which boats have now reached such wonderful dimensions and efficiency, mainly through the improvement of engine weight per h.p. Our flying boat engines were 125 h.p. Austro-Daimler weighing somewhere near 1000 lbs.

Yours very sincerely

(Signed) Douglas White

R.L. Charteris   Learned to fly at the Deperdussin School at Brooklands and obtained his Royal Aero Club Certificate (No.197) on 12 March 1912. He became a pilot for the All British Engine Company (A.B.C.) and was to have flown one of the Avro Biplanes in the 1912 Military Trials. However, the engine was not finished in time.

E.C. Gordon England   Born at Concordia, Argentina, in 1891. He first became involved with aviation when he went to help Noel Pemberton-Billing at Fambridge. Whilst there he met Jose Weiss, who was testing his tail-less monoplane and he subsequently went to Amberley in Sussex, where he test flew, although without previous experience, Weiss's glider. Gordon England continued testing Weiss's powered monoplanes at Brooklands and also flew an Hanriot. Early in 1911 he joined the Bristol School at Brooklands and gained his Royal Aero Club "ticket" (No.68) on 25 April 1911. He was immediately taken on to the staff of the Bristol School of Flying as an instructor and flew at Filton, Salisbury Plain and Brooklands. He very soon showed aptitude as a designer and produced plans for several aeroplanes built by Bristols during 1911/12. Two of his designs were entered for the 1912 Military Trials; one the machines he piloted himself.

In 1913, he joined James Radley, first at Huntingdon and then at Shoreham, and helped design two versions of a large waterplane. He worked with Radley on the construction of the annular-wing monoplane, designed by Cedric Lee and G. Tilghman Richards. During its first flight on 23 November 1913, it was piloted by Gordon England who found, shortly after take-off, that it was tail heavy. It thereupon stalled and crashed from about 150 feet, luckily without injury to the pilot. At the same time he became a freelance test pilot and designer and worked for J. Samuel White at Cowes, where he tested the Wight seaplanes. Much of the test flying of the early White & Thompson machines was carried out by Gordon England.

In September 1915 he became pilot and consultant designer for Frederick Sage & Company, Peterborough, an old-established firm of shopfitters, who had just been offered a contract by the Admiralty to build Short 184 seaplanes. He eventually became manager of the factory.

Wilmot Sitwell Nicholson was promoted Captain on 30 June 1909; on 17 December 1912 he was appointed Captain of H.M.S. *Dreadnought* and on 1 August 1914 captain of the armoured cruiser *Hogue*, one of three cruisers sunk by the German submarine *U-9* within a single hour in September 1914.

He was promoted Rear-Admiral, commanding the 2nd Light Cruiser Squadron in June 1921 and retired as a Vice-Admiral in November 1925.

He does not appear ever to have gained a Royal Aero Club certificate.

John Lankester Parker   Born at Barton Mills, Suffolk, in 1896; he was partly crippled following an attack of polio as a child. He trained as a pilot at the Vickers School, Brooklands, in 1913 and was awarded his Royal Aero Club Certificate (No.795) on 28 May 1914. He worked as an unpaid instructor and mechanic at the Beatty School at Hendon and on the outbreak of war he volunteered for the R.F.C. but was not accepted owing to his disability. He therefore went to the Northern Aircraft Company at Windermere as an instructor on waterplanes. After the takeover of the School by the R.N.A.S. he went to Shorts at Eastchurch and tested their large Bombers and then to Rochester to test seaplanes. At the same time he worked as a freelance test pilot for Norman Thompson. On one occasion, whilst making a ferry flight in mid-winter from Middleton, the tail came off the flying boat and it came down in the sea. Parker spent eight hours clinging to the wreckage before being picked up.

Clifford B. Prodger   An American, he learned to fly in 1915 at the Beatty School. Early in 1916 he set up a test-flying partnership with the Australian Sydney Pickles. In the same year he became a test pilot for Handley Page and flew the second prototype O/100 and subsequently the V/1500. Lankester Parker joined the partnership as an additional freelance pilot.

Frederick P. Raynham   was born in 1892 and gained his Royal Aero Club "Ticket" (No.85) on 9 May 1911 at Brooklands. He subsequently became an instructor at the Avro School. At the beginning of 1912 he joined the Sopwith Company as a test pilot and in July he was engaged by Howard Flanders to test his monoplanes and deliver them to the R.F.C. at Farnborough. At the 1912 Military Trials he flew the Flanders monoplane and Coventry Ordnance biplane. He subsequently rejoined A.V. Roe and gained considerable experience on the Avro seaplane at Shoreham and Brighton. He ferried a dozen of their machines to Farnborough and Eastchurch. This experience proved invaluable when he went to work for Norman Thompson as a freelance.

E.R. Whitehouse joined the Aeronautical Syndicate at Hendon as a pupil to learn aircraft construction. He subsequently went to the Deperdussin School at Hendon and qualified as a pilot on 21 January 1913 (Royal Aero Club Certificate No.407). He continued to fly for the Deperdussin Company and then went on a three-month tour of Britain to demonstrate the Handley Page monoplane.

At the end of August 1913, he went to White & Thompson to fly the No.1 Biplane and subsequently returned to Handley Page.

APPENDIX X

James Linfield & Sons Ltd., New Road, Littlehampton

The old-established (1882) building firm of James Linfield carried out all the major construction work for White & Thompson and The Norman Thompson Flight Company at Middleton.

They still retain their old account books which show the following contracts:

October 1914	New hangar	£ 875.00
	Canvas front	£ 60.00
	Engine house	£ 94.00
	Office extension	£ 64.00
	Wave screen (sea wall?)	£ 235.00
	Sundry work	£ 57.00
Nov/Dec 1914	Sundry works	£ 213.00
January 1915	Sundry works	£ 280.00
July/Sep 1915	Tube store	£ 45.00
	Sheet piling	£ 106.00
	Sundry works	£ 50.00
Oct/Nov 1915	Concrete wall	£ 125.00
	Tube work shed	£ 220.00
	Garage and cycle shed	£ 190.00
	Engine test shed	£ 209.00
	Timber shed	£ 155.00
	Sundry works	£ 100.00
Nov/Dec 1915	Lavatories	£ 66.00
	Sundry works	£ 254.00
Jan/Mar 1916	Sundry works	£1214.00
April/Sep 1916	New buildings	£7207.00
December 1916	Sundry works	£ 966.00
Jan/June 1917	Sundry works	£ 830.00
July/Aug 1917	Sundry works	£ 150.00
Sep/Dec 1917	Sundry works	£ 469.00
Jan/Feb 1918	Sundry works	£ 41.00

Two of the aircraft erection shops built by Linfield had clear span roofs of 90 feet and 130 feet respectively support by Belfast trusses and Linfields still have the original drawings of these and other buildings at Middleton.

APPENDIX XI

Letter from Murray Sueter to Porte 20.2.17

Air Dept.
20.2.17

My dear Porte,

On leaving the Administrative side of the Air Service for more active service in Mediterranean I felt it my duty to write to express to you my high appreciation and admiration for the big effort you have made to develop the Boat type seaplane.

From the first moment I saw a float type in the Air I was convinced that the solution of the Seaplane problem lay in developing the Boat type.

As you know my Assistant Director and Technical Adviser opposed the Boat type for all they were worth and you alone supported me in developing the type, for this I have to thank you.

The whole R.N.A.S. owe you much for tackling the problem in so successful a manner and when I say your Boat type Seaplane must have saved very many Pilots' lives I do not think I exaggerate.

Well good luck Porte, and may your health permit you to continue for a long time in your work is the wish of

Your friend and admirer

Murray F. Sueter

ACKNOWLEDGMENTS

I do not apologise for repeating the sentiment that I expressed at the beginning of the acknowledgments in my Wight Aircraft book, viz:

One of the most pleasant rewards for the author of a book of this type comes from the great kindness and enthusiastic help which is received from a host of individuals and organisations and also from the numerous new friendships that are made during the course of research. It is with great pleasure that I take this opportunity of recording the names of those who have made this history possible.

Foremost among them is Oliver Norman Thompson who entertained me most lavishly and gave me total access to all his father's remaining papers and photographs and searched his memory for interesting recollections of his father's career.

The story would be a much poorer thing without the fascinating tales of the Royal Naval Air Service recalled by Professor Sir Austin Robinson, who had actual experience of flying Norman Thompson flying boats and was able to give me a first-hand account of these machines, "warts and all".

The following former employees of the company and residents in the Bognor and Littlehampton area were kind enough to search their memories and their homes for information and photographs: David Ames, Ron Iden, Phil Linberry, R.Linfield (Jas.Linfield & Sons), Peter Marrett, E.N.Montague, Alexander Newland, E. Robinson, H.J.F.Thompson.

I owe a special debt of gratitude to the following little band of aircraft historians and enthusiasts who have offered me much encouragement and advice over the years and who have given me complete and unselfish access to their own collections of historical material and photographs. In addition they have, in several cases, allowed me to quote from their own published works: Barry Abraham, John Bagley, C.H.Barnes, Dick Barton, J.M.Bruce, P.T.Capon, Lew Casey, Peter Cooksley, H.F.Cowley, Barry Gray, Philip Jarrett, Ken Molson, Graham Mottram, Ces Mowthorpe, Harald Penrose, Bruce Robertson, A.V.Stephens, Bert Tagg.

As always, Jack Bruce and Stuart Leslie were unstinting in the provision of photographs from their unrivalled collection.

I must also thank John Sizer, Ian Stair and Cliff Minney who produced the excellent three-view drawings, often from very scanty material.

Finally I must express my appreciation for the helpful advice and assistance which has been given me by the staff of the following organisations and without which my task would have been almost impossible: Royal Air Force Museum, Fleet Air Arm Museum, Imperial War Museum, Public Record Office, British Museum Newspaper Library (British Library), the Patent Office, The Science Museum, Bognor College Library, Coventry (Lanchester) Polytechnic Library, Royal Aeronautical Society Library, National Reference Library of Science and Invention, The Companies Register, Somerset House, Ministry of Defence (Naval Historical Library).

My thanks are also due to Paul Leeman and other members of the Cross and Cockade Society for their help in various ways.

AIR-BRITAIN - THE INTERNATIONAL ASSOCIATION OF AVIATION HISTORIANS - FOUNDED 1948

For forty-eight years, Air-Britain has recorded aviation events as they have happened, because today's events are tomorrow's history. In addition, considerable research into the past has been undertaken to provide historians with the background to aviation history. Over 15,000 members have contributed to our aims and efforts in that time and many have become accepted authorities in their own fields.

Every month, *AIR-BRITAIN NEWS* covers the current civil and military scene.

Quarterly, each member receives *AIR-BRITAIN DIGEST* which is a fully-illustrated journal containing articles on various subjects, both past and present.

For those interested in military aviation history, there is the quarterly *AEROMILITARIA* which is designed to delve more deeply into the background of, mainly, British and Commonwealth military aviation than is possible in commercial publications and whose format permits it to be used as components of a filing system which suits the readers' requirements. Also published quarterly is *ARCHIVE*, produced in a similar format to *AEROMILITARIA* but covering civil aviation history in depth on a world-wide basis. Both magazines are well-illustrated by photographs and drawings.

In addition to these regular publications, there are monographs covering type histories, both military and civil, airline fleets, Royal Air Force registers, squadron histories and the civil registers of a large number of countries. Although our publications are available to non-members, prices are considerably lower for members who have priority over non-members when availability is limited. Normally, the accumulated price discounts for which members qualify when buying monographs far exceed the annual subscription rates.

A large team of aviation experts is available to answer members' queries on most aspects of aviation. If you have made a study of any particular subject, you may be able to expand your knowledge by joining those with similar interests. Also available to members are libraries of colour slides and photographs which supply slides and prints at prices considerably lower than those charged by commercial firms.

There are local branches of the Association in Blackpool, Bournemouth, Central Scotland, Exeter, Gwent, Heston, London, Luton, Manchester, Merseyside, North-East England, Rugby, Sheffield, Southampton, South-West Essex, Stansted, W. Cornwall and West Midlands. Overseas in France and the Netherlands.

If you would like to receive samples of Air-Britain magazines, please write to the following address enclosing 50p and stating your particular interests. If you would like only a brochure, please send a stamped self-addressed envelope to the same address (preferably 230 mm by 160 mm or over)

Air-Britain Membership Enquiries (Mil), 1 Rose Cottages, 179 Penn Road, Hazlemere, High Wycombe, Bucks., HP15 7NE

MILITARY AVIATION PUBLICATIONS

Royal Air Force Aircraft series: (prices are for members/non-members and are post-free)

J1-J9999	(£8.00/£12.00)	K1000-K9999	(£2.50/£3.75)*	L1000-N9999	(£12.00/£18.00)
P1000-P9999	(£2.00/£3.00)*	R1000-R9999	(£2.50/£3.75)*	T1000-T9999	(£3.00/£4.50)*
V1000-W9999	(£4.00/£6.00)*	X1000-Z9999	(£4.00/£6.00)*	AA100-AZ999	(£6.00/£9.00)*
BA100-BZ999	(£6.00/£9.00)	DA100-DZ999	(£5.00/£7.50)	EA100-EZ999	(£5.00/£7.50)
FA100-FZ999	(£5.00/£7.50)	HA100-HZ999	(£6.00/£9.00)	JA100-JZ999	(£6.00/£9.00)
KA100-KZ999	(£6.00/£9.00)	LA100-LZ999	(£7.00/£10.50)	MA199-MZ999	(£8.00/£12.00)
NA100-NZ999	(£8.00/£12.00)	PA100-RZ999	(£10.00/£15.00)	SA100-VZ999	(£6.00/£9.00)
		WA100-WZ999	(£5.00/£7.50)*		

Type Histories

The Halifax File	(£6.00/£9.00)*	The Lancaster File	(£8.00/£12.00)*	The Washington File	(£2.00/£3.00)*
The Whitley File	(£4.50/£6.75)*	The Typhoon File	(£4.00/£6.00)*	The Stirling File	(£6.00/£9.00)*
The Anson File	(£15.00/£22.50)	The Harvard File	(£7.00/£10.50)	The Hampden File	(£11.00/£16.50)
The Hornet File	(£9.00/£13.50)	The Beaufort File	(£10.00/£15.00)	The Camel File	(£13.00/£19.00)

Hardbacks

The Squadrons of the Royal Air Force and Commonwealth (£15.00/£22.50)
The Squadrons of the Fleet Air Arm (£24.00/£36.00)
Fleet Air Arm Aircraft 1939 - 1945 (£24.00/£36.00)
Royal Navy Shipboard Aircraft Developments 1912 - 1931 (£15.00/£22.50)
Royal Navy Aircraft Serials and Units 1911 - 1919 (£15.00/£22.50)
Central American and Caribbean Air Forces (£12.50/£18.75)
The British Aircraft Specifications File (£20.00/£30.00)
The K File - The Royal Air Force of the 1930s (£23.00/£30.00)

Individual Squadron Histories

Strike True - The History of No.80 Squadron, Royal Air Force (£4.00/£6.00)*
With Courage and Faith - The History of No.18 Squadron, Royal Air Force (£5.00/£7.50)
Scorpions Sting - The History of No.84 Squadron, Royal Air Force (£11.00/£16.50)
Rise from the East - The History of No.247 Squadron, Royal Air Force (£13.00/£16.50)
* Currently out of print

The above are available from Air-Britain Sales Department, 5 Bradley Road, Upper Norwood, London SE19 3NT
Access, Visa, Mastercard accepted